The great thing about Steve Bull's insights is that they stay with you. They provide an array of practical things to do that demonstrably drive team, individual and one's own performance.

**Trevor Bish-Jones,
CEO of Woolworths plc**

Steve Bull's work has played a significant role in the England and Wales Cricket Board's recent success both on and off the field.

**David Collier,
CEO of the England and Wales Cricket Board**

Steve Bull has made a huge contribution to the recent success of Olympic sport in the UK. His unique and sensitive approach has led to an increase in performance by individual athletes, teams and his fellow professionals alike in the most demanding of all sporting environments, the Olympic Games.

**Simon Clegg,
CEO of the British Olympic Association**

Steve Bull has an incredible depth of knowledge and his ideas are constantly stimulating and challenging. I admire the way he so easily presents practical models that can be applied in the workplace every day.

Tony Holmes,
Wholesale Director, Coca-Cola Enterprises UK

For the last five years, Steve Bull has translated lessons learned from coaching high performance athletes into first class development programmes that have created real and lasting impact for our organization. Mental toughness is a skill set that can be learned, can be put into action immediately, and which is critical for unleashing potential in our competitive, hard driving business environment.

Kim Steckley,
Global Head of Succession Management,
Roche Pharmaceuticals

Steve Bull enthused and inspired me in a way that has been the single most impactful intervention in my 16 year business career.

Paddy Dummett,
People & Organizational Development Manager,
Marie Curie Cancer Care

THE GAME PLAN

Your Guide to Mental Toughness at Work

STEVE BULL
Consultant psychologist to the England cricket team

CAPSTONE

First published 2006 by
Capstone Publishing Limited (a Wiley Company)
The Atrium
Southern Gate
Chichester
West Sussex
PO19 8SQ
www.wileyeurope.com
Email (for orders and customer service enquires): cs-books@wiley.co.uk

British Library Cataloging in Publication Data
A catalogue record for this book is available from the British Library

ISBN 13: 978-1-84112-725-5
ISBN 10: 1-84112-725-6

Typeset in ITC Garamond 12/16pt by Sparks – www.sparks.co.uk
Printed and bound in Great Britain by TJ International Ltd, Padstow, Cornwall

This book is printed on acid-free paper responsibly manufactured from sustainable for-
estry in which at least two trees are planted for each one used for paper production.

Substantial discounts on bulk quantities of Capstone Books are available to
corporations, professional associations and other organizations. For details telephone John Wiley & Sons on (+44) 1243–770441, fax (+44) 1243 770571 or email
corporatedevelopment@wiley.co.uk

To Alexa and Morgan
who help keep me focused
on the important things in life

PARK LANE COLLEGE
HORSFORTH CENTRE LIBRARY
Calverley Lane, Horsforth, Leeds LS18 4RQ Tel: 2162440

This book must be returned by the latest date shown.
Please bring the book with you or telephone if you wish
to extend the period of loan. Short loan books are not
renewable.
FINES WILL BE CHARGED ON OVERDUE BOOKS.

Contents

Acknowledgements

As is usually the case, there are many people to thank, but first and foremost has to be my wife Donna, who supported my schedules throughout the process as well as providing really helpful comments on earlier drafts of the manuscript. To my parents, Perce and Mary, who were the first to educate me about the value of resilience and mental toughness. John Moseley, from Capstone, who showed a real enthusiasm for the idea of the book from the early stages. Michael Atherton, whose memorable performance against South Africa at Trent Bridge in 1998, and my subsequent conversations with him about it, kick-started my interest in conducting a rigorous investigation into the various components of mental toughness. Hugh Morris, Deputy Chief Executive of the ECB, who has provided endless support for my consultancy work in cricket. Robin Mills, from Woolworths, who gave up his time generously to be interviewed for the book and with whom I have enjoyed many informative hours of discussion and debate on the connections between winning in sport and business. And finally, the many other athletes and executives with whom I have worked over the years who have helped shape my thinking on the psychology of performance generally.

Foreword

I'm always trying to think about how we are going to improve and move to the next level or how I am going to get that little bit extra out of a player. Steve Bull has provided excellent advice and support in helping me to do this. During 2004 I was playing badly and I knew I had to do something to regain my form. I started seeing Steve on a one-to-one basis and we worked on techniques to help clear my mind and relax more. I respect his professional approach and his expertise in the psychology of performance. Mental toughness is critical in top level sport and I am sure that it's essential for success in business too. Steve Bull's ideas and techniques will equip anyone in business with a game plan for acquiring the winning edge.

Michael Vaughan, OBE,
Captain of the 2005 Ashes winning England Cricket Team

Beginning with the Ashes in Mind

In the summer of 2005, the England Cricket Team regained the Ashes by beating Australia in a five match series, which has been described by many experts as the greatest series of all time. The ebbs and flows of each game were captivating, even to the non-cricket follower. The margins of victory were invariably desperately small. The pressure was immense throughout. Mental toughness played a crucial role from the opening minutes of the first day at Lords to the final climax at The Oval on 12 September. Going into this fifth match, England were winning 2–1 and needed at least a draw to regain the trophy that had eluded them for the previous 18 years. In his weekly column preceding the start of the match, *Sunday Telegraph* cricket correspondent Scyld Berry wrote:

> *The Fifth Test starting at the Oval on Thursday can absorb any superlative you care to throw at it. The biggest sporting occasion in Britain since 1966; the most important cricket match ever played in England, and the most significant anywhere if it ends up ending the Australian empire; and the climax of the most exciting Test series of all time.*[1]

Scyld Berry, *Sunday Telegraph* cricket correspondent

So, under these extreme conditions, how were the players feeling going into this match? How did they prepare? How confident were they? How did they manage to stay focused on the right things? How did they deal with the pressure of expectation from the media and the public – not to mention that which they were placing on themselves? If you were advising those players in the lead up to the game, what would you have said? It's too easy to simply say 'be positive – have confidence'. As Simon Barnes once wrote in his piece in *The Times*:

> *Confidence is a bar of soap in the power shower of the sporting life. Grasp it too tight and it squirts from your hands; reach to pick it up again and you are flat on your back.*[2]

Simon Barnes, *The Times*

We know that under pressure people can sometimes find a few extra percent and perform above their natural levels. Equally, and perhaps more commonly, some individuals simply fall apart when the pressure is on and experience the dreaded 'choke' – a word that is banned from being uttered in many sporting locker rooms for fear of the psychological impact merely thinking about it can have. The England Cricket Team had been accused of choking many times in previous years but something was different about the 2005 team. They demonstrated a degree of mental toughness and resilience which had been absent in the past. Their 'attitude' was different and as Jonny Wilkinson once said:

That sort of attitude training, mental toughness if you like, can be the difference between winning and losing. What you want to develop is the kind of mentality that says, in the last five minutes of a game when the score is tied, 'Give me the ball' rather than 'I wish this was all over, I can't do any more'. Winners and losers are made right there.[3]

Jonny Wilkinson, member of 2003 World Cup winning England rugby team

This new found 'attitude' demonstrated by these England cricketers did not, however, suddenly emerge at the start of the summer in 2005. As the old cliché goes … it takes five years to create an overnight sensation. Performances on the field during the summer of 2005 had been the result of years of hard work and quality preparation which had begun when Nasser Hussain took over the captaincy in 1999 and set about creating a different kind of 'environment'. When Michael Vaughan was appointed captain in 2003, he continued to raise the bar until eventually England were in a position to present a realistic challenge to the Australian team which had occupied a pre-eminent position in world cricket for more than a decade.

In short, in 2005 England had a 'game plan' and each individual player going into that famous deciding match at the Oval knew exactly what he needed to focus on in order to maximize his personal contribution to the team effort. They were not going to get carried away with the enormity of the occasion because they would be focusing on their own individual 'performance processes' over which they could exert personal control. They would be totally prepared for all eventualities and feel absolute confidence in the knowledge that they had not left any stone unturned. They had established a 'framework' for success which, although not guaranteeing victory, would certainly give them the best possible chance. And as Andrew Flintoff said at the conclusion of the series:

> *They say that victory goes to the side that wants it more. That's an old cliché and it's not true. Victory goes to the side that prepares the best.*[4]

Andrew Flintoff, England cricket all rounder

This book is about winning – but not on the sports field. It's about winning in business. It's about 'you' winning in business. It's about 'your' personal performance at work. It's about how you can create a 'personal performance environment' that enables you to deliver at the crucial times. The book will help you create a 'game plan' which will give you the type of mental toughness required to be a high performer in the ever more pressurized world of corporate life in the 21st century. This is a world which is demanding, dynamic and driven. Mental toughness is essential if you are to 'thrive' rather than simply 'survive' in a culture which increasingly expects you to deliver more whilst spending less. The book will explore different types of mental toughness and examine how knowledge of each can give you the platform for significantly increased levels of self-confidence and resilience. Whatever your position or role in a company, there will be tips and advice in the book for you. The approaches I shall outline are those that I have found to be most successful in my business consultancy working with individuals ranging across the company spectrum from CEOs to new recruits. The content of the book is based around a model of mental toughness which I developed out of a piece of mental toughness research I conducted in my role as England Cricket Team Psychologist. As well as working directly with the England Team itself, this role has also involved running the Leadership strand of the England and Wales Cricket Board's Elite Coaches' Development Programme and has thus given me the opportunity to work closely with a wide range of high quality coaches as well as international players.

In 1996, I wrote a book called *The Mental Game Plan: Getting Psyched for Sport,* which provides the reader with a user-friendly guide to using mental skills in competitive sport. In the opening pages of that book, I asked the question, 'What is this thing we call mental toughness?' and proceeded to outline a number of attributes demonstrated by tough performers such as high self-belief, staying positive in the face of pressure and having an extremely strong desire to succeed. Two years later I was working with the England Cricket Team during a summer in which they were playing against South Africa. England had not won a major Test series for over a decade and were 0–1 down in the series with two matches to play. The fourth match was played at Trent Bridge and it provided one of the most memorable periods of fierce competition between two players – Michael Atherton (who was batting) and Allan Donald (who was bowling). It was an awesome spectacle to watch as Donald peppered Atherton with a series of extremely fast and hostile deliveries. As the episode unfolded, spectators became aware that this personal battle would probably decide the entire five-match series. If Donald got Atherton out, South Africa would most likely win the game and hence the series 2–0 with a match still to play. If Atherton could hang on, and fend off Donald's attack, England could win the match, level the series, and go to Headingley with a chance of sneaking an unlikely series win. The critical period of play lasted just under an hour. Atherton managed to hang on, see Donald off, and England won the match. They went to Headingley and won there too, claiming an unlikely series victory which is still remembered for that 60 minute hostile and aggressive interchange displayed at Trent Bridge. Some time after the series, I was still, as a psychologist, fascinated to reflect on Atherton's performance and arranged to interview him at length about how he coped with the demands and pressure of the situation. That conversation sparked an interest in researching the area of mental toughness generally in cricket. I was becoming increasingly frustrated with supposed experts who were liberally using the term to label players without actually understanding what it was and how it could be developed. I wanted to understand mental toughness from the perspective of those who had 'been there and done it' in order to ascertain what we could learn to help our younger players be 'fast tracked' to a position of superior mental resilience. At the same time, I was very encouraged to hear from Atherton that although he felt some people were naturally tougher than others, it was a skill that could be worked on and improved.

I think some people have natural mental toughness and some people don't but I do think that it can be acquired and you can work to get better at it.[5]
Michael Atherton, former England cricket captain

I proceeded to survey over 100 cricket coaches asking them who they thought the toughest England players of the 80s and 90s were and then simply compiled a ranking list to identify the most appropriate players to approach. Knowing most of them personally, I was then able to conduct an in-depth interview with 12 of the top 15 ranked players. The list was a veritable 'who's who' of English cricket and included Graham Gooch, Mike Gatting, Nasser Hussain, Darren Gough, Alec Stewart and of course Michael Atherton himself (who was incidentally ranked No. 1 by a considerable margin!).

The results of this study were published in the national press but in the course of conducting the interviews and analysing all the data, I began to formulate a model that had wider ranging implications beyond cricket. It appeared that mental toughness was not as straightforward as many people would think and could even be categorized into different types requiring different 'mindsets' for different situations. The model that emerged appeared easily applicable to other sports. I began reflecting on the experience I have had of working at three Olympic Games as Great Britain Headquarters Psychologist. During these events, I had observed how athletes, and indeed team managers, coped with the multi-faceted pressures which are so evident in the Olympic environment. I had seen mental toughness at its best and at its worst. I began reviewing all I had learned over the previous 20 years working in elite sport. During that time, in addition to my work in cricket, I had consulted with performers from the professional tennis circuit, the European PGA golf tour, both the English Soccer and Rugby Union Premierships, professional motor sport, the British Ski Team, the British Equestrian Team, the British Track and Field Team and many others.

Pulling all this material together, I then set about creating a model that would add value to my executive coaching in the corporate world. I tested the model with many individuals across a wide range of very different blue chip organizations in both the UK and the United States. Although the corporate context varies enormously between these companies, the challenges facing individuals seem to me to be remarkably similar. People are challenged with working long hours, have to perform under extreme pressure much of the time and must deal with constant change, adversity and setbacks. Confidence, clear thinking and resilience are prerequisites for success and will discriminate between winning and losing in the same way that they will in sport. It is my observation that many people in corporate life do not fully appreciate that they are 'performing' and hence would benefit from a 'performance mindset' in dealing with their job demands. Consider the following situations that people encounter during their day-to-day business life:

- conducting a one-to-one performance appraisal,
- making a presentation to the board,
- meeting a new client in a situation where it is crucial that a good impression is made,
- getting through a hectic 12 hour day which includes travel, several meetings, a working lunch and report writing,
- running a team meeting,
- presenting a monthly progress report to colleagues.

This list could go on and on but my point is that these challenges are 'performances'. Not in the sense of a Shakespearian play but in the sense of an athletic performance. They require focus, confidence, resilience, quick thinking and the ability to deal with distractions and pressure. In other words, they require 'mental toughness'. This being the case a great deal can be learned from the attributes and behaviours of the elite, mentally tough, sports performer.

In summary, the notion of the 'corporate athlete' as originally described by Jim Loehr and Tony Schwartz several years ago, is resonating more and more with the business clients I come across these days. Individuals need a 'game plan' to help them prepare for, cope with, and learn from, the pressures they are facing in everyday corporate life. This book presents a framework for that 'game plan'. I hope you enjoy it and I'm confident that if you apply the principles and techniques outlined you will significantly increase your prospects of winning in business by developing your mental toughness.

What is this Thing We Call Mental Toughness?

Winning is about individuals performing when it gets tough, not when it's easy.[1]

Michael Vaughan, Captain of the 2005 Ashes winning England Cricket Team

It's not easy

Corporate life is tough these days – tougher than it was in previous years. Just as performance standards have increased dramatically in elite sport, so they have in business. Working hours are long, the demands are relentless, and the technology age, which has given us the capacity to communicate so quickly and efficiently, has simply piled on the pressure. So let's make one thing clear from the start – performing at your best is not easy. If it were, we'd all be doing it a lot more often. Performing under pressure is tough and requires a mental approach that does not come naturally to many people. Fear, anxiety and poor emotional control are the default position for many in the corporate world ... but not for winners. Winners have the capacity to enter challenging situations with confidence and a sense of excitement. They enjoy the buzz of having to execute quality performance against the odds. They love the 'great white heat' of competition and seem to thrive on the pressure occasions. How do they do this? How do they stay focused? How do they remain calm? How do they display such a strong sense of self-belief when the circumstances appear so dreadful and intimidating? Answer – they are mentally tough. But what does that term mean? What is this thing we call mental toughness? The model that I've created in recent years is based on 20 years of work as a psychologist in elite sport and 10 years of corporate consulting as an executive coach. The model has been tried and tested in all sorts of different environments and will help you develop your winning edge by becoming more mentally resilient. The basic premise of the model is rooted in the importance of 'thinking' in the performance process. As a sport psychologist, I have been fortunate to make a living for the past 20 years out of being a 'mind coach' to athletes. This does not negate or trivialize the role of physical or technical abilities. Quite the opposite in fact. I maintain that if you get your mind right then you are simply allowing yourself the opportunity to display your natural talents to the best of your ability. Mind skills are not a substitute for other talents but rather the prerequisite for achieving optimal performance levels by coping effectively with the pressure of the situation. This is true whether it be on the playing field, in the concert hall, in the boardroom or in the office.

The mental strength is so important ... there's no limit if you're prepared to get in there and fight it out.[2]
Duncan Fletcher, Coach of the 2005 Ashes winning England Cricket Team

The power of the mind is an accepted fact these days and there are libraries of books devoted to the topic. Many of these books, however, are quite long, involved and generic. I want this book to be 'punchy' and focused on the business environment. I want you to be able to read this book quite quickly and hence start using the ideas straightaway. The model I am about to introduce you to is not complicated, even though it is derived from many years of research and consultancy. It will help you to think more clearly about the pressures and challenges you are facing and put realistic plans in place to allow you to 'raise your performance bar'.

A model of mental toughness

The following examples illustrate the kind of challenges which face people working in business and serve to introduce the various dimensions of the model upon which this book is based.

Mental Toughness Scenario 1: Geoff – 35-year-old marketing manager

Geoff is a confident guy who has had many successes during his time working in three different organizations over the past 12 years. However, the team that he manages has failed to deliver against its targets this year and Geoff is feeling responsible for the disappointing performance. Added to this, he has recently received a poor performance appraisal from his boss which ranked as the worst he has ever had. He is feeling very down about the current situation and is aware that his confidence has taken a beating. He and his team have a tough time coming up in the next few months and he knows that he will need to be resilient and tough to deal with all the impending pressures that are inevitable. But he can't seem to get positive about things and he is struggling to regain his usual confidence. Each day seems to present another potential disappointment and Geoff knows that he must break this cycle of negativity in which he finds himself.

Geoff needs to turn things around in his own mind before he does anything else. He has to display mental toughness for his own good and for the benefit of his team. In short, Geoff needs some coaching on **Turnaround Toughness**. This is the first part of the mental toughness model and is all about regaining self-belief when things are going badly. Turnaround Toughness is about dealing with adversity and setback. It's about coming back strong when things seem to have gone against you. We've all experienced this challenge at certain points in our lives. How do we regroup and focus on a positive approach for moving forward? Consider these specific situations:

- Bouncing back after failing to gain a much-deserved promotion.
- Staying positive when working for an unsupportive or critical boss.
- Maintaining commitment to your organization when facing the imposition of unrealistic performance targets by senior management.
- Sustaining self-belief when you have performed poorly in the last few team meetings and received feedback about your lack of constructive contribution.
- Getting some really bad luck at a time when things needed to go your way.

How do you cope with the pressure these situations create? You must reconnect with your previous performance accomplishments and make sure that you approach your future challenges with a confident mindset that focuses on success and achievement rather than failure and disappointment. The world of elite sport is packed full of stories exemplifying this type of mental approach and Turnaround Toughness.

The two Olympic Golds and six world titles may go down as the defining statistics of my career, but I am more proud of making the most of my limited talent and never refusing to believe I wasn't going to win at the Olympics – even after missing the 1992 Games through injury and those in 1996 due to illness the day before I was due to race.[3]

James Cracknell, Double Olympic Gold Medallist

James Cracknell had more than his fair share of ups and downs during his amazing career as an international rower – including being part of Steve Redgrave's team which famously won Gold (Redgrave's fifth) in Sydney in 2000. The quote above illustrates how Cracknell demonstrated Turnaround Toughness after having to deal with the disappointment of missing out on both the Barcelona and Atlanta Olympics before finally getting his chance in Sydney.

Mental Toughness Scenario 2: Laura – 28-year-old sales executive

Laura is a talented salesperson who regularly exceeds her annual targets. She is a confident extrovert who loves the challenge of influencing customers and closing deals. Her interpersonal communication skills are very strong and she is highly regarded for her contributions to team meetings. However, next week Laura has to make a presentation to the senior management group for the first time. She knows that two of the executives to whom she will be presenting are well known for their harsh views about the sales team as a whole and although Laura has been performing well, she knows that this will not count for much in this particular situation. She is nervous about the presentation and is concerned that she may blow her opportunity for impressing the key decision makers in the organization. At the back of her mind she knows that she can do it but she is becoming increasingly anxious about all the things that could go wrong in the ten minutes she will be 'on stage' presenting.

Laura is aware that her performance in this meeting will be closely scrutinized and that her reputation within the company will be significantly influenced by how she does. She has the ability to execute an excellent performance but she has to be focused and clear in the manner of her delivery. Laura needs some coaching on **Critical Moment Toughness**. This is the second part of the mental toughness model and it is about nailing something within a specific performance context. The golfer sinking the final putt to win on the 18th green. The footballer drilling the penalty kick to win the game. The tennis player serving an ace to save a match point. It's about holding your nerve under pressure. It requires clear thinking and a positive focus. You don't necessarily have to deliver anything out of the ordinary. Sometimes it's simply delivering your normal thing under more demanding circumstances. In sport we sometimes talk about the 'clutch' situation and the fact that it can separate champions from contenders. As Simon Barnes wrote in *The Times* in 1995:

> *The classic example is the two foot putt. Even the non-golfer can knock in two-foot putts. But could we do it for a bet of a million pounds? Or when the Ryder Cup depends on it? Most of us could walk along the kerb without a hint of concern about falling into the gutter. But supposing the kerb was 3000 feet off the ground? Not so easy. And that is what a clutch situation means.*

Now consider these specific 'clutch' situations in your world:

- Clinching a big sales deal when you know you will only get this one chance and you think the customer has lost interest.
- Conducting a difficult one-to-one appraisal meeting when you know the other person is set on catching you out.
- Making an important presentation in front of a large audience when you don't like public speaking.
- Bumping into the CEO in the elevator and having a two minute opportunity to impress.
- Performing your best during a job interview for a position in a company you have always wanted to work for and knowing that this is your one big chance.

So how do you get yourself into the 'zone' as the athletes say? How do you create the kind of mindset that will give you the best possible chance of nailing the performance? You must engage in quality preparation involving focusing on the key processes which will set you up for success and ensuring that you maintain emotional control throughout the performance. Sounds easy doesn't it? Sounds like common sense. That's because, to a large extent, it *is* common sense. But … I often refer to performance psychology as 'a set of common-sense principles not commonly applied'. There's no weird and wonderful stuff involved. It's basic, down-to-earth common sense much of the time. But we know that people have a tendency to forget the basics when they are under pressure or feeling stressed.

You always have these thoughts creeping into your head, a picture of how things might not work out. The biggest challenge sometimes is getting rid of those mental pictures and putting positive things in there. If you can get

*away from that and avoid that, in any part of your life,
it makes a huge difference.*[4]

**Roy Halliday, American League
baseball top pitcher in 2003**

Roy Halliday explains the simplicity of focusing on positive processes and emphasizes how important this is in all walks of life. It is not, however, something that people tend to be naturally good at – particularly when facing a clutch situation and needing to demonstrate Critical Moment Toughness.

Mental Toughness Scenario 3: Paul – 41-year-old IT specialist

Paul works for a software company that is undergoing significant change with the prospect of a merger in the coming months. Staff reductions have led to a situation whereby he is having to cover two jobs for a three month period. This requires him to have an office base in London and another in Leeds. His travel schedule has become a major issue in recent weeks involving him being away from home far more than he would wish and clocking up many extra miles on the motorways and trains. He is starting to feel chronically tired and run down and seems to be getting more than his fair share of coughs and colds. He is under pressure to add the odd visit to Brussels into his already packed schedule but he is worried that this will push him over the edge. His boss is not overly sympathetic and simply advises him to delegate more and organize his time efficiently. Paul has two colleagues who seem to cope quite well with similar schedules and who often appear far more energetic than he ever feels, contributing more to team meetings and coming up with innovative ideas which have impact. Paul feels that he is simply keeping his head above water.

Paul is struggling with the 'road warrior syndrome'. He is travelling excessively and not coping well with the demands this is placing on his body. He is probably getting dragged into far too many meetings and consequently finding that his performance is suffering as well as his health. He *must* take serious action and could benefit from some coaching on **Endurance Toughness**. This is part three of the mental toughness model. It's about staying healthy and performing well even when you are excessively fatigued or stressed due to the relentless demands of your job and the culture within which you are working. Travel and time away from home exacerbate this problem. Many people suffer from the road warrior factor even if they are only having to deal with a daily commute which can be severely draining on energy levels. Anyone who has experienced the 'adrenalin soaked rush hour dash' will relate to this I am sure. Staying physically strong and being able to think clearly when you are extremely busy and tired at the same time is very much part of the mental toughness package. Think about these situations:

- Rushing into a business meeting straight after a long flight or car journey and having to be on top of your material immediately.
- Having to perform at work when you are feeling exhausted due to the demands of parenting a young child at home.
- Staying healthy when you have to travel twice as much as your monthly average whilst working the same number of hours.
- Maintaining a relaxed state when you are disrupted by travel issues such as flight/train delays or motorway traffic that causes you to be late for your meeting.
- Coping with the feelings associated with a loss of the work-life balance that you have been striving for in recent times due to your job demands whilst the company restructures.

How do you deal with this type of pressure? How do you keep yourself physically robust and healthy? How do you maintain the levels of high performance that you are aiming for when you are feeling so tired and stressed out? You must manage your energy levels by adopting a healthy lifestyle which will need to include adequate attention to physical activity, nutrition and relaxation.

After a Test match the body is tired and the mind is drained.[5]

Andrew Strauss, Ashes winning
England Cricketer

Andrew Strauss describes how weary cricketers are after playing a Test match but the fact is they often have very little time to regain their mental and physical energy for the next big match. It's therefore critical that they stay in good physical shape and concentrate on eating the right foods that will not only give them energy but will also enable them to concentrate better as well. The England Team now uses a Consultant Nutritionist to advise the players in these matters as well as the full-time Fitness Coach and Physiologist Nigel Stockill who has worked, and travelled, with the team for the past six years. As with the other aspects of the mental toughness model, the basic principles of Endurance Toughness are the same regardless of the context. In addition to looking after the body, it's also important to look after the mind and, therefore, Paul will benefit from some coaching on managing his outlook as a way of coping with the relentless demands he is facing.

Mental Toughness Scenario 4: Karen – 36-year-old buyer

Karen is a buyer for a retail company in London. She has been in her current role for three years and although she is well respected and enjoys working for the organization, she has always felt that her style is overly cautious and that she would raise her performance significantly if she could push herself into difficult situations more often and take some riskier options. She finds it hard to make tough decisions and tends to default to the safe option, which invariably delivers acceptable – but not exceptional – performance. She greatly admires one of her colleagues who seems able to make the tough calls and go for the risky option even when the stakes are quite high. Karen has several opportunities coming up in the next few months to adopt a new approach but is not confident that she will 'seize the day'.

Karen could benefit from talking to some of the elite athletes I have worked with over the years. These individuals demonstrate an amazing capacity to make difficult decisions under pressure and know exactly when to take the risky, versus the safe, option. They demonstrate high levels of **Risk Management Toughness**, which represents the fourth part of the mental toughness model. Many Olympic medallists inhabit a world where they find themselves in situations where they cannot afford *not* to take a risk. Although this is a double negative statement, it distinguishes from risks that simply *can* afford to be taken but do not necessarily *need* to be. The most extreme example of this distinction is illustrated by the quote below from Lesley McKenna, Britain's most successful snowboarder to date.

Unless you risk everything, you're not going to finish in the top 10 anyway.[6]

**Lesley McKenna, Great Britain Olympic snow-
boarder**

Now, this quote is somewhat extreme and I am absolutely *not* recommending that you adopt this attitude on a general basis, However, there are times when taking the risky option is the mentally tough thing to do and the skill is in recognizing the occasions when this is the case and then having the confidence to make the decision to 'go for it'. Consider these challenges:

- Having the confidence to challenge your boss about a decision they have made, which you think may need reconsidering.
- Being bold enough to speak up in a meeting when you are new to a team and still feeling your way.
- Taking personal responsibility for something that has gone wrong rather than seeking to find blame elsewhere.
- Applying for a promotion which you think you deserve but feel that you don't have a chance of getting and you are hence concerned that you will look foolish by registering your interest.
- Taking a risky option on a deal which could lead to a large profit or a large loss depending on the outcome.

Each of these situations demands a certain type of Risk Management Toughness whereby you would need to be totally clear in your mind of the right decision to make and then have absolute faith in your ability to live with the consequences. This is part of mental toughness and I am sure that you can think of friends, colleagues and athletes who are particularly good at this type of mindset. How can you develop your capacity to make these difficult decisions and take the risky option provided the time is right? You need to have high levels of self-awareness – knowing your strengths and limitations. You need to be able to appraise the relative demands of a situation accurately and you need to be capable of thinking clearly when in a pressure situation. You also need to be good at maintaining perspective – appreciating that the bigger picture consequences of not succeeding are rarely as bad as we may think.

It's not the end of the world. My dog will still lick my face whether I win or lose.[7]
Matt Biondi, US swimmer – after losing his Olympic title in 1992

So there it is. The four basic components of mental toughness. **Turnaround Toughness** representing the ability to bounce back from adversity and setbacks. **Critical Moment Toughness** being the ability to execute a performance at a specific time when under pressure. **Endurance Toughness** referring to being able to stay physically strong and mentally focused during times of excessive stress, relentless workload commitments and perhaps a heavy travel schedule. **Risk Management Toughness** representing the ability to make tough decisions and take the risky option in order to maximize performance gains rather than playing safe and hence missing out on real opportunities for significant success. The following four chapters of the book will now explore each of the components in more detail and provide tips on how to develop your mental toughness skills.

Mental toughness is the capacity to maintain self-belief, clear thinking and resilience when under relentless pressure to deliver optimal performance.

The Mental Toughness model on the following page also shows how each of the four components will contribute to the enhancement of three factors which are directly related to peak performance – (1) self-belief, (2) clear thinking and (3) resilience. You can see how the four mental toughness types contribute to these factors in the representation of the model overleaf. Although I'm not hugely in favour of presenting a formal definition of 'mental toughness', because I believe it to be multi-faceted, if I was pushed into doing so, my definition would be focused around these three factors – i.e., maintaining self-belief, clear thinking and resilience when under relentless pressure to deliver optimal performance.

Using this book

The book is written in a way that does not require it to be read in order. You may wish to go straight to the section on Critical Moment Toughness or Endurance Toughness. Although some cross-referencing does exist, it will not present a problem to you in working through the sections out of sequence. Also, you may feel that all four of the toughness types are not relevant to your own performance challenges and you may decide to focus on just two or three. This is fine, although I would strongly encourage you to cover all of the sections at some point as you never know when you may need to draw on the specifics of each mental toughness component. A new job, new responsibilities, new challenges are all possibilities in the future so, forewarned is forearmed as the old saying goes!

And finally, I will conclude this section with the first of ten tips I am going to give you throughout the book.

Mental toughness model

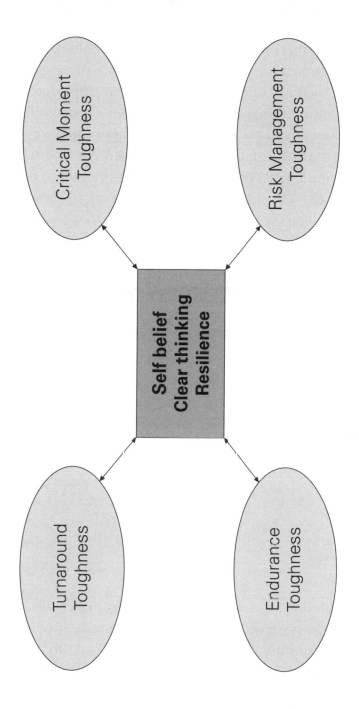

TIP 1: ADOPT AN 'ATHLETE MINDSET'

I concluded the introductory section by challenging you to think of yourself as a performer. Remember the examples I gave you such as conducting a one-to-one appraisal, making a presentation to the board or creating an impact with a new client. These are all 'performances' and hence require the type of mental approach that comes naturally to the elite athlete. In simple terms I shall encourage you to think of three phases of performance – (1) preparation, (2) execution, (3) review. Let's present that in a cyclical form …

The performance cycle

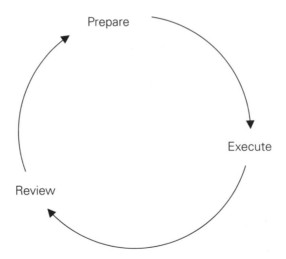

Prepare

Execute

Review

In my experience of corporate consulting over the past ten years I have observed the same 'performance' phenomenon in every organization in which I have worked, irrespective of business sector. These sectors have included fast-moving consumer goods, banking, retail, pharma, IT, law, public services and leisure. The common challenge is that of 'pace'. Everyone is under pressure to get things done quickly. We live in a 'solution-focused' culture these days. Action, action, action. There is little time to pause for breath. And so what I observe is individuals 'lurching' from one performance to the next. Rushing from one meeting to another. Using lunch as an opportunity to squeeze in another client review or one-to-one appraisal. I have even come across one senior manager in a company who consistently began work at 5am each day and then proceeded to arrange breakfast, lunch and dinner appointments with clients five days a week. Yes ... that's 15 client meetings per week and an average working day of 15–16 hours!

This kind of pace inevitably militates against engaging in quality preparation or review either side of a performance. Hence my use of the term 'lurch' when I describe people moving from one performance to the next. People miss out two of the elements in the performance cycle. The message has to be 'slow down a little and take the time to prepare for events and then review them afterwards'. View this as an investment of time rather than a cost, as I am convinced that in the long run you will recoup this time by enhancing your performance.

The techniques and strategies I shall give you in this book will involve some planning and require you to spend time that you probably feel you don't have. That is precisely why I need you to adopt an 'athlete mindset' and accept that in order to develop your mental toughness you will need to devote quality time to creating a personalized 'game plan'. Once you have this plan you will be amazed at how it will impact on your attitudes, behaviour and performance. I've helped you as best I can by keeping the tips simple and user-friendly. There is no complicated theory in any of the book's sections – just common sense.

So, to summarize Tip 1. View yourself as an athlete – albeit not one who spends huge chunks of their life in a gym and who performs in a stadium watched by fans. You are, nevertheless, performing for much of your working day and need to tune in to how your mental approach will influence these performances. This makes quality preparation beforehand, and quality review afterwards, absolutely critical in the whole process. Consider how you could apply Eric Cantona's quote about preparation to your own performance environment:

> *Preparation is everything. Focus is the key. The concentration has to be exactly right. It's easy to battle it out on the pitch without having prepared fully and then say, 'I gave it my all'. The point is that if you had prepared carefully you would have had more to give and you'd have played better.*[8]

> **Eric Cantona, former French international soccer player**

Now consider the same for what Tiger Woods says about the importance of review.

> *My goal at the end of each tournament is to look back and say what can I learn from it.*[9]

> **Tiger Woods, arguably the greatest golfer of all time**

An athlete mindset involves accepting that lurching from performance to performance is not conducive to maximizing potential – you really do need to focus on how you prepare for an event and what you can learn from it afterwards. By making preparation and review part of your game plan, you will enhance your mental toughness by:

1 Increasing your **self-belief**.

2 Demonstrating **clear thinking** much more often and especially in pressure situations.

3 Becoming more **resilient**.

Imagine that some time in the future you feel significantly stronger in these three areas than you do right now. You have higher self-belief, you think more clearly under pressure and you demonstrate the kind of resilience that allows you to cope with challenge more positively and bounce back from disappointment better. Your business performance would improve and you would have, what we call in sport psychology, a 'winning mind'. Even if you rate your mental toughness pretty highly right now – I guarantee there is room for improvement. That's another element of the 'athlete mindset'. We call it constructive dissatisfaction. Whatever your level of performance currently, there is a need to raise the bar. The world is constantly changing and performance levels are continuing to increase.

In top level sport it is the mind games that make the difference between the good and the outstanding.[10]

**Stuart Barnes, former rugby international and
SKY Sports commentator**

The quote by Stuart Barnes articulates a view held by most people who work in elite sport. Getting your mind right cannot be underestimated if winning is your aim. The same is true in corporate life these days. Attitude and mental strength are so often the key differentiators between success and failure. Consider the emergence of emotional intelligence over the past decade and how it is now widely accepted as a critical element in a manager's portfolio of attributes. Daniel Goleman's groundbreaking book *Working With Emotional Intelligence*, published in 1998, opened with a chapter entitled 'The New Yardstick'. Consider the quote taken from it below:

> *The rules for work are changing. We're being judged by a new yardstick: not just by how smart we are, or by our training and expertise ... People are beginning to realize that success takes more than intellectual excellence or technical prowess, and that we need another sort of skill just to survive – and certainly to thrive – in the increasingly turbulent job market of the future. Internal qualities such as resilience, initiative, optimism and adaptability are taking on a new valuation.*[11]

Professor Daniel Goleman, from his bestselling book *Working with Emotional Intelligence*

Resilience, initiative, optimism and adaptability are closely related to mental toughness and they are attributes which need to be constantly worked on. There is always more stuff to learn and new challenges to face. Elite athletes are constantly on the lookout for how they can improve their 'mental game' even if they are reigning world champion. They know that if they stand still too long, they will soon be overtaken. They prepare meticulously and they engage in quality review processes to check what they can learn along the way. This is the mindset of the athlete and the challenge to adopt it is Tip 1.

Turnaround Toughness

Success doesn't always go in a straight line. You're going to cop these things. It's how you cope with set-backs which is the sign of a good team.[1]

Clive Woodward, former England Rugby Coach in 2001 after England had failed for the third time to win the Grand Slam. Two years later they famously won the World Cup.

Kelly's story

When Kelly Holmes won her two Gold Medals at the Athens Olympics in 2004 it was the culmination of a ten year period of ups and downs. Her journey had begun in 1994 when she won Commonwealth Games Gold and European Championships Silver in the 1500 metres. The following year she won Silver in the 1500 metres and Bronze in the 800 metres at the World Championships. She then suffered a stress fracture to a foot during the build-up to the Atlanta Olympics and missed out on a medal by coming fourth in the 800 metres. In 1997 she then went to the World Championships as favourite to win but injured her Achilles tendon and ruptured a calf pulling out of the 1500 metres. She was out of action for a year. She came back in 1998 to win Silver in the 1500 metres at the Common-wealth Games. All was set for the Sydney 2000 Olympics two years later but ten weeks before the Games started she tore a calf muscle. Amazingly she recovered and managed to win a Bronze medal in the 800 metres. The following year she was struck down by chronic fatigue syndrome (a debilitating illness supposedly related to the Epstein-Barr virus). She recovered and won Gold again at the Commonwealth Games in 2002 and Silver at the World Championships in 2003. As the record books show, she then made history by winning a double Gold in the 800 and 1500 metres events at the Athens Olympics. I remember sitting in the stands watching Kelly during those Olympics and then seeing her in the Athletes' Lounge after she had won her medals. She appeared humble, approachable and even quite shy but behind these outward signs there was obviously an incredibly mentally tough and resilient performer. She had shown that it is possible to come back strong after adversity and the way in which she had dealt with all her injuries and setbacks clearly illustrated her Turnaround Toughness skills.

The Ashes 2005

The England Cricket Team were confident going into the five match Ashes series in 2005. Each player was very aware that this was the best opportunity of beating Australia they had had for over 15 years. The team had experienced a very success-ful 3 years leading into the Ashes series and now was the time to nail the big one. I can clearly recall the atmosphere around the locker room and the practice ground in the days leading up to the start of the first match. It was tense but there was a feeling of anticipation and excitement. So much so, that one could sense the impatience among the players.

We do not fear playing them and we are actually looking forward to what is a massive challenge.[2]
Michael Vaughan, England Captain

They simply wanted to 'get started' and were ready to take to the field at least a day early.

Everyone knew how important the first period of play was going to be. The first two hours … the first 30 minutes … the first 5 minutes … even the first ball. It was crucial that England got the upper hand and showed Australia that they meant business. The outcome … a superb start. Steve Harmison, England's opening bowler, set the tone with a hostile opening spell which laid down a mark of intent from this new England team. It was exactly the start England had wanted and Australia were bowled out for 190 runs – a poor total by any standards. England had not begun an Ashes campaign this well for years and spirits were high. However, Australia's strike bowler Glenn McGrath then proceeded to bowl an immaculate spell triggered by taking his 500th wicket in Test cricket. England were 92 runs for seven wickets at the end of the first day and in a deep hole. They went on to lose the match and the daggers were out in the media. The team was written off and the chants of 'here we go again' could be heard up and down the country. Overnight, people had lost faith in the team and felt that Australia were set to retain the Ashes once again. However, the view within the team was quite different. It was time for Turnaround Toughness. It was time to stay confident and look at the bigger picture. One game lost – four to play. The series was still very much alive and everyone associated with the team had to believe this. I gave a number of media interviews during the week following that first Test match and my message was the same in each one. 'The players will be reconnecting with the previous successes they have experienced together. They will be focusing on their strengths and confirming in the minds just how good they are. They will learn from this match but return for match two in a confident and energized state of mind. This *is* a mentally tough team.'

I told them we had ten days to regroup: don't pay any attention to the rubbish that will be written, be strong, make sure we come back as a fresh team, one that is ready to have another go. People were saying when we went 1–0 down that we'd lost the Ashes already, but that wasn't the case.[3]

Michael Vaughan, England Captain

In his book, *Calling the Shots*, Michael Vaughan explains how he made sure that the positives from the first match were highlighted in the players' minds despite the match being lost. This is exactly the right approach to take in these situations and is clearly an important element of Turnaround Toughness.

I just emphasized the positives. The start we made was positive; Pietersen's debut had been impressive and Harmison's bowling outstanding so there was nothing to be too downhearted about ... We'd come back before and I was confident we would do it again ... Mentally I remained strong despite my poor start. I wasn't going to read the rubbish in the press; instead I focused on the positives.[4]

Michael Vaughan, England Captain

So what's the message here? What must you do when you are experiencing a difficult time? How do you go about bouncing back from disappointment, poor performance or simply rotten luck? Let's look at Tip 2.

TIP 2: RECONNECT WITH PREVIOUS SUCCESSES

It seems to be a human frailty that we are programmed to focus on failure and disappointment far more than on success and accomplishment. We find it very easy to recall those disastrous days when everything went wrong and we were left feeling embarrassed and incompetent. When next faced with a similar challenge our brains are quick to recall the previous catastrophe and regenerate those awful feelings of despair and anxiety. This type of thinking, of course, sends us into a spiral of negativity resulting in a loss of confidence. We are then trapped in the cycle of low confidence contributing to poor performance which merely results in further damage to our self-confidence and even more disappointing results. The cycle must be broken and the most effective way of doing this is to actively reconnect your mind with previous accomplishments. This, of course, does not come naturally and so we need a tool to help us.

The Confidence Peaks Chart

The figure on page 34 shows a blank version of this simple tool. You will see the representation of a mountain range with 12 peaks.

The way in which I shall use this tool is to encourage you to imagine that each of the peaks represents a significant achievement that you have accomplished in the past. Reflect on these achievements and record each on one of the mountains in the chart. Think hard and dig deep. It may not come easily but I am sure that if you really focus your mind you will be able to generate 12 achievements of which you are genuinely proud. The next figure provides a sample chart which may help you in getting started. You will see in this sample that the confidence peaks cover a wide range of areas dating back to school days.

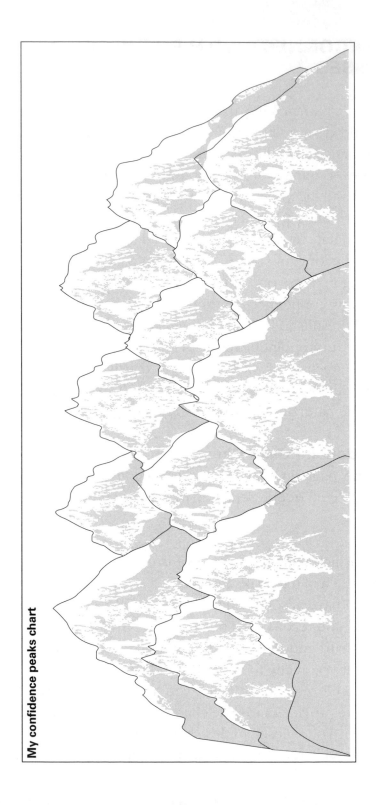

My confidence peaks chart

Sample confidence peaks chart

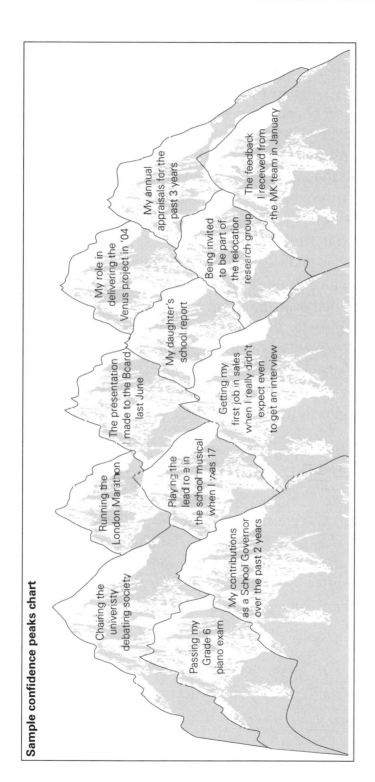

Chairing the univeristy debating society

Running the London Marathon

My role in delivering the Venus project in '04

My annual appraisals for the past 3 years

The presentation made to the Board last June

My daughter's school report

Being invited to be part of the relocation research group

The feedback I received from the MK team in January

Passing my Grade 6 piano exam

Playing the lead role in the school musical when I was 17

Getting my first job in sales when I really didn't expect even to get an interview

My contributions as a School Governor over the past 2 years

Some are related to work and others are focused on family or outside interests. This is referred to as a 'General' Confidence Peaks Chart. You could also use the tool to focus more specifically on a set of achievements that are directly related to a particular challenge that you are currently dealing with or perhaps a chart relating to a difficult three months that you know you are about to embark on and which will inevitably involve setbacks and frustrations. This would be a 'Specific' Confidence Peaks Chart. Both types are useful and will assist enormously in developing your Turnaround Toughness. It looks like a really simple technique and it is! But my experience with it has been uniformly positive. It presents you with the evidence of how you have climbed many mountains in your life. Some of these have been big peaks and others have been small. They have all been achievements though and remind you how you have conquered challenge and adversity. The more you go through life the bigger your mountain range becomes and the platform for your self-belief establishes a firmer and firmer base.

The trick is to remember the good moments and use them when you face a challenge … you don't want to be recalling crap; you want to recall the good stuff.[5]
Nick Faldo, six times Major winner and Britain's greatest ever golfer

I've used the confidence peaks chart in many different forms over the past 20 years in both sport and business. It works most effectively when the individual, in addition to merely describing the achievement, recalls as much detail about the event as possible – how they were feeling, what they were thinking, how they behaved. The principle here is that the process of 'reconnection' will be that much more powerful if the achievement can be remembered in all its glorious detail.

Gilo's story

England cricketer Ashley Giles (nicknamed Gilo) has spoken very publicly about how this Tip 2 helped him through the lowest point of his professional career. In 2004, Giles was suffering a run of bad form and was receiving relentless criticism not only from the media but from England supporters as well. He suffered so badly that before the third Test against New Zealand he seriously considered retiring from the sport. He is quoted as saying, 'There comes a time when you feel no one actually wants you there, so why keep doing it?' In an article published in *The Wisden Cricketer* magazine in October 2004, Giles recalled the meeting he had with me during that summer and the impact it had had on him:

> *My head was pounding. I just said to him, 'I really need to speak to you'. So we wandered out for a coffee in the afternoon. I know Bully quite well anyway, he's a pretty down-to-earth bloke, and I think even he was surprised at how I was feeling. I got everything out and we chatted about it, reaffirming how good I am and what I have done, the good things I can do for the side … And that's really been the turning point. Steve Bull has turned it round for me. From that next day the moment the ball was in my hand I felt a different animal.*[6]

Ashley Giles, Ashes winning England cricketer

Ashley is very kind in his acknowledgement of the help I gave him but I have to say that it was fairly straightforward advice which essentially focused on a version of the Confidence Peaks Chart. I challenged him to start talking about the following three things …

1   His previous accomplishments as an England player.
2   His natural talents and strengths as an international per-
    former.
3   The extra value that he added to the current England side
    in terms of his professionalism, commitment and attitude.

Not only did we talk about these things but I actively encouraged him to make notes and construct a version of the Mountain Range in the form of a diary and performance log. The
impact of this approach on him was evident very quickly as
he stated and most notably a few weeks after he had reconnected with his accomplishments and his strengths he famously
conjured a ball to Brian Lara (one of the best players the world
has ever seen) which sent his stumps flying. The video footage
capturing the reaction of Giles and his team-mates is memorable. Mission accomplished. A player suffering from severe
loss of confidence and having to deal with extreme pressure
had been reconnected with his previous successes and remembered what he was good at. He had regained his identity as
a performer and was full of self-belief. He now knew that he
had Turnaround Toughness and that he may well need to use
this again some time in the future. As it happened, following
the defeat against Australia in the first 2005 Ashes match, Giles
experienced a relapse. The press were on his back again and
one headline read 'Why playing Giles is akin to taking the field
with only ten men.' In other words the view being expressed
was that England would do better if they dropped Giles and
were a player short. Understandably, Giles was hurt by this – so
much so that he locked horns with the press and challenged
them back. This did not prove to be an effective strategy in
the end and so Giles, once again, returned to the technique of
reconnecting with his previous successes. And again, the technique worked as he was to go on and play an instrumental role
in the team winning the Ashes series.

Kate's Treasure Box

Other athletes apply the confidence peaks principle in different ways. The former Canadian World Champion skier Kate Pace explained her version in the form of a Treasure Box.

> *I took out a piece of paper and started writing down all the good things in my life, all the things that made me feel good. I ended up with about eight pages of stuff, like my family, my friends, all the people who supported me, all of my successes, all of the times I had overcome injuries … I wrote on my race evaluation form, 'Today you built a treasure box'. In that treasure box were all the good things in my life. Every time I would get that feeling like I wasn't very confident anymore, I'd try to remember the treasure box and all the things I put in it. I'd take out some of those things at the bottom that didn't really fill me up anymore and put new stuff on top. When I'd be riding up the lift to the start, I'd imagine that treasure box and I'd just imagine opening up the lid and all those good things in there.[7]*

> **Kate Pace, former Canadian World Champion skier**

In the 1990s I worked with the British Ski Team for five years and was always interested to gain ideas from athletes from other nations – particularly given that British skiers were always at something of a disadvantage having to constantly travel to the Alps to find snow and mountains on which to practice. I can recall hearing Kate reflect on her career in a presentation once and it transpired, as is so often the case, that she had had to endure significant setbacks and disappointment throughout her career. She repeatedly used the phrase 'climbing on adversity' and even suggested that she would not have been successful without it. She claimed that the adversity and all the injuries taught her how to bounce back and win over and over again by applying the right type of 'thinking'.

The Confidence Account

I sometimes liken this process to a 'personal confidence bank account'. Every time you are able to reflect on your successes and reconnect in some way with a previous success you are making a deposit in your confidence bank account. Over time, you will build up a healthy balance which will be really useful in the future when your confidence is a little shaky and you need to make a withdrawal from the account. If the balance is healthy there is plenty to withdraw. If, however, you haven't been regularly making the deposits then come withdrawal time you may be struggling. It therefore makes sense to keep your Confidence Peaks Chart topped up as Kate Pace explained when discussing her treasure box. In sport, I would encourage an athlete to revisit their 'General' chart at least once a season and I find every 6–9 months a good time frame for business people. Clearly 'Specific' charts are created as necessary depending on the challenge being faced.

Nick's story

Nick Brookes is the Cold Channel Director for Coca-Cola Enterprises in the UK. I have worked with Nick as his coach for the past four years as part of the company's Leadership Development programme which was delivered by Lane4 Management Group – the performance consultancy run by Olympic Gold Medalist Adrian Moorhouse. In partnership with the HR function of CCE, the programme received 'Best Executive Development Programme' at the 2004 Annual HR Awards held at the Dorchester Hotel in London. During this extensive programme, when the Lane4 coaching team introduced the company's senior managers to the area of self-belief, we spent considerable time on helping them use techniques for reconnecting with previous accomplishments using the same principles as those I have described for the Confidence Peaks Chart – i.e. reconnect with your successes when self-belief is low. Nick Brookes utilized the approach in a powerful way with his team as a whole. Here's his story in his own words:

Our team had suffered a series of significant setbacks after three very successful years. We had lost two major contracts, worth millions in turnover, to a competitor in a matter of weeks, two more major customers had moved outlet supply from direct delivery to a wholesale source making the impact of the sales team difficult to measure without the data and by the end of the first quarter of the year the budgeted volume and profit targets which had been challenging, but readily accepted, at the start of the year were beginning to look daunting. The impact on the team was to sap morale and confidence and it became noticeable in monthly team meetings and individual one-to-ones that people were seeking to blame others to rationalize performance rather than think positively and to seek solutions to fill the gap. This created a self-fulfilling vicious circle.

The Executive Group of the senior managers in the channel decided to adopt two key strategies to address the issue. The first was to engage in a complete review of the trading strategy for the channel over the next three years. This required an analysis of all the available data both internal and external, a series of interviews with senior managers in the key accounts to confirm the current performance of the company and the team, an external benchmarking exercise to provide an independent view of how they ranked versus the competitors in meeting the needs of the customers and then a series of internal stakeholder interviews to ensure that any future strategy delivered against their objectives.

However, this review would take several weeks to complete and although it would set a clear vision for the future the more immediate issue was the morale and confidence of the team. So, the second strategy was to combine a regular brand-briefing meeting with a reminder of the team's past successes. Ahead of the meeting each team member, including the senior managers, had to submit a single chart highlighting some previous success that they were particularly proud of and the reason why. At regular points during the meeting individuals were selected at random and asked to present their success. This was then placed on a wall of the room and over the course of the meeting built to an impressive array of past success. But the exercise also served as a great energizer during the meeting and kept the atmosphere extremely positive. Following the meeting all these 'victories' were collected and tidied up and a massive poster produced which was displayed on a wall in the office around the hot desk area the account team used. This served as a reminder that there was enormous talent in the team and that even under severe pressure they were capable of delivering great results.

I visited the company's offices just outside London to coach Nick almost two years after the team had conducted this exercise. It was fascinating to witness the massive poster still attached to the office wall after all that time – serving, as Nick says, to remind the team of the enormous talent it has and how capable it is of delivering results when under pressure.

So remember, the process of reconnecting with previous successes is not just a technique for individuals – it works for teams as well.

TIP 3: LEARN AND MOVE ON

Experiences of disappointment, adversity or poor performance are invariably unpleasant. However, mentally tough performers are able to extract positives from them by doing two things extremely well – (1) learning something and (2) moving on and focusing on the next challenge. Doing this can often be very difficult though – especially when your mind cannot seem to rid itself of the negative memories associated with the experience. People talk about 'leaving it on the wave behind' but is it really that easy? Well, here's a story about heart surgery which may help you understand the process a little better.

A surgeon's story

Heart surgery is a situation where a human life actually depends on how well a person 'performs'. In the mid 1990s Dr Curt Tribble, a cardiothoracic surgeon based at the University of Virginia School of Medicine presented some fascinating insights into the 'psychology' of learning about, and conducting, heart surgery. I remember hearing Dr Tribble deliver a presentation at the World Congress of Mental Training in Ottawa during which he spoke about the challenges of teaching young resident doctors the skills of conducting a coronary bypass. He explained how in previous years he had become interested in the similarities between the everyday demands placed on athletes and surgeons and proceeded to outline his approach to coaching surgical skills. His main point was that, as a young resident doctor, you had to learn on the job – so to speak. You would be coached by an experienced surgeon, such as himself, who would provide feedback to you as you conducted an operation. The challenge was how you would process this feedback, learn from it and move on to the next phase of the surgery. He presented a simple, yet incredibly powerful, approach for guiding young surgeons' thinking – 'Remember and Forgive'. He claimed that any performer, but surgeons in particular, should utilize these three words when dealing with demanding situations where high performance is essential but where you may have to deal with suboptimal outcomes along the way. In short, you must learn quickly from your mistakes but then move on to the next challenge as soon as possible. Don't get bogged down in dwelling on the previous suboptimal performance. Either change it, if you can, or learn something and move on. The quote below, which is taken from an article published in the *Journal of Performance Education* illustrates the point powerfully.

> *'The main thing we do is to sew a graft which connects a vein onto an artery. They're pretty small. They're about the size of the inside of a ballpoint pen ... It takes about 25 stitches for an anastomosis. And we're going to do about four of these per patient. Every stitch has a specific technique. Every one is different. Every one of them counts, but some count more than others ... Basically, as you move along you've got to be able to remember what you're doing, you need to learn what you're doing, and then you've got to forgive yourself. You've got to be able to move on. You've got to blank it out of your mind. In that precise window of each of those 25 stitches, the person must process what they see themselves and what I tell them. They have to be able to place the stitch, think about it for about a second, decide in their own mind if they liked it, listen to whether I liked it or not, and decide whether to accept it or reject it. Is it*

good enough or not good enough? Do they need to take it back out and reposition it? ... In that window, the person has to learn to do it, evaluate it, learn from it, and then blank it out. Because if it is still hanging over you, if you've still got that baggage, when you put the next stitch in, it will affect the whole operation. The previous stitch you put in may not cause that much trouble. It may not be quite right – some comment may have been made about it, you're thinking about it. However, you have got to blank it out completely or the operation is shot. You've got to learn, then forget. Learn, absorb it all, get it back, move on ... That can apply to everything in life ... Forgive and remember. You learn from it and you move on from there ... Prepare, learn, forgive, and move on.' [8]

Curt Tribble, M.D., cardiothoracic surgeon

Athletes have to adopt 'learn and move on' thinking or else they get stuck in thinking about past events. It's crucial for athletes to engage in what we call a 'here and now focus'. This means paying attention to the relevant cues for right now and what is immediately coming up. If they are a second behind on this it's usually too late and a mistake has been made.

It's not dissimilar in your world. You cannot fall into the trap of dwelling on an error and replaying it in your mind. Learn something positive from it and then move on. You must refocus on the 'here and now'. This is mental toughness and the performance benefits are obvious.

'This is one thing I say to my residency applicants. "Having gone through your record, as far as I can tell you have never failed at anything. You've been a great

student, a great athlete, you've accomplished all these things, and you probably have not experienced failure, at least not in its ultimate, bitter, full boring way. You are going to have things that are not going to work well. How are you going to deal with that reality?" They usually don't have a plan.' [9]

Curt Tribble, M.D., cardiothoracic surgeon

The Game Plan for Turnaround Toughness

- Compile a General Confidence Peaks Chart and keep it topped up by repeating the process every 6–9 months.

- Read through your Peaks Chart on a regular basis to stay closely connected with your performance accomplishments.

- Create another blank Peaks Chart which you can use for specific situations such as those described in the opening section of the book.

- When you are faced with a setback or any experience which erodes your confidence remember to revisit your Peaks Charts and reconnect with your successes and achievements.

- Memorize the 'learn and move on' mantra. Think about situations in which having 'learn and move on' thinking will be particularly important and then implement it as often as you can.

Critical Moment Toughness

We knew that those last two sessions on Saturday could be series defining. If they won to go 2–0 with three to play then our chances would have been slimmer than a catwalk model. We had to win.[1]

Michael Vaughan, recalling the Second Ashes Test at Edgbaston in 2005

Great athletes relish these 'clutch' situations. It is not unusual for them to become defining moments in a career. Jonny Wilkinson clinching the last minute dropped goal to win the Rugby World Cup in 2003 springs to mind. It can, of course, work the other way. Chris Waddle will be forever remembered for missing the crucial penalty shoot-out kick in the semi-final of the 1990 World Cup. Likewise Jean van de Velde's dramatic faltering in the 1999 Open Golf Championship. The pressure of these situations can sometimes be intolerable for spectators let alone the performers themselves. Experiencing the 'choke' is a traumatic event for any athlete – as entertainingly described by Matthew Syed.

No sportsman can honestly claim total immunity to the choking phenomenon and the experience is uniformly disturbing. My personal battles with it have followed a now familiar pattern. First is the conscious realization that the pivotal moment in the match has been reached. This is followed by an irresistible quickening of the heart, a slight trembling of the hands and then the catastrophe – I abruptly depart from that realm of instinctive sporting interaction, where the mind effortlessly processes relevant information and disregards the superfluous. In short, I leave the zone. [2]

Matthew Syed, Commonwealth Games Champion Table Tennis Player

I mentioned earlier in the book that the mere mention of the word 'choke' is banned from many sporting locker rooms. Why this is the case is demonstrated by a fascinating piece of research conducted by Professor Larry Leith which was published in the *International Journal of Sport Psychology* in 1988. The title of the paper was 'Choking in Sports: Are We Our Own Worst Enemies?' Leith was convinced that the very thought of the prospect of choking would be enough to induce it and set up a study whereby he took a group of university students and split them in half. Both groups were then asked, one by one, to carry out a basketball shooting challenge. The instructions given to each group, although delivered separately, were identical in all but one respect. Group 2 were told, just as they were about to go and perform, that there was a phenomenon in sport called 'choking'. It was explained that this was a very serious thing if it happened and that often someone's performance demonstrated a catastrophic drop when choking occurred. They were therefore advised *not* to choke. The results? The group who were given the choking information performed significantly lower than the group who were only given the basic instructions. Leith had been proved correct. The mere thought of choking had been enough to effect a change in performance.

'Bottling it' generally refers to the same phenomenon. Not delivering the goods at the critical time. Fluffing your presentation, losing your focus in a meeting, getting tongue-tied during an interview, completely losing your confidence when attempting to challenge your boss about an issue – these are all examples of 'lost nerve'. And it happens to talented people in all walks of life.

David Cameron's story

In 2005 Michael Howard, the leader of the British Conservative Party stood down from his position and a keenly contested battle for his successor began. The final two candidates were David Davis (the early favourite and Shadow Home Secretary) and David Cameron (the young pretender with less than five years' experience as a Member of Parliament). It is widely agreed that the turning point in the leadership campaign was reached at the annual party conference in Blackpool. Days before the conference began, each candidate launched his manifesto in London but the contrast in style was clear. The delivery from Cameron was relaxed but polished. He spoke without notes although the apparent spontaneity was evidently based on extensive preparation revealed by a video obtained at the time by the *Daily Telegraph* newspaper. At the conference itself, Cameron again was relaxed, free flowing, but extremely impactful. He nailed it. In contrast Davis admitted that he 'fouled up' his speech by not paying enough attention to it. In an interview with Sky News, he claimed that he had been so busy appearing at fringe events and meeting party members that he did not concentrate properly on his speech. The result – he did not demonstrate Critical Moment Toughness and paid a very high price for it. Tom Bradby, ITN's political editor, claimed that the speech by Davis had 'bombed and bombed badly'. Cameron on the other hand did two very basic things right. First, he recognized how important these 'moments' in time were going to be. Second, he prepared for them – to the point whereby his preparation was so good that he gave the impression of performing 'off the cuff'. Planned spontaneity, as we like to call it in performance psychology.

These two things enabled David Cameron to display Critical Moment Toughness which clearly had a demonstrable effect on his performance.

My big speech let me down through lack of concentration, Davis admits.[3]

The Times 25.10.05

A 2005 survey of over 600 executives conducted by the Chartered Management Institute showed that four out of ten conceded they had taken decisions against their better judgment after being pressured or bounced into making panic commitments. Getting things wrong in these critical moments can, and does, cost the company large amounts of money. How does mental toughness help? It can assist in enabling someone to stay focused on the right things at the right times. Let's look at the two tips for developing your Critical Moment Toughness that I'm suggesting in this section. Once again – there's no complicated science here. Just applying those commonsense principles that get forgotten in the heat of the moment when the pressure gets turned up.

TIP 4: CONTROL THE CONTROLLABLES

The old adage 'control the controllables' is unquestionably the most commonly used phrase in the world of sport psychology. I will often advise athletes that if they don't remember anything else about our conversation, be sure to remember this one phrase. It is invaluable. Why waste energy, effort and resources in worrying about, or getting angry about, uncontrollable factors such as poor weather, inferior equipment or the experience of the opposition. I advise athletes to focus on the things they can do something about. The quote by Lawrence Dallaglio is a perfect illustration of this mindset.

> *We have to concentrate on the elements we can control.*
> *We are only human, some things are beyond us: I can't*
> *control the weather, I can't control the referee (although*
> *sometimes I may have tried!), or the bounce of the ball.*
> *But what you can control is your own performance.*[4]

Lawrence Dallaglio, member of the 2003 World Cup winning England rugby team

Alex Coomber may not be a familiar name to you but she was an unlikely medallist at the 2002 Winter Olympics in Salt Lake City. Great Britain rarely wins medals in the Winter Games but Alex won a Bronze in the bob skeleton event – that's the one that has been likened to hurtling down a mountain on a tea tray! Look at what she said in the days leading up to her Olympic final. Her attitude is a perfect lesson for anyone entering into a challenging situation where the odds are against them.

You have to go back to the adage 'control the controlla-bles'... whether people do well or badly, I have no control over. The only thing I can control is myself, my equipment and my performance, and that's what I'll do.[5]

**Alex Coomber, Bronze Medallist
at the 2002 Winter Olympics**

The former England cricketer Graham Thorpe is regarded by some as the finest batsman of his generation. He played in 100 Test matches scoring 6744 runs. The latter part of his illustrious career was dogged with personal problems emanating from the breakdown of his marriage but throughout all the ups and downs he was always acknowledged as an extremely mentally tough competitor. I recall many interesting conversations with him over the years about mental toughness and was always impressed with his steely determination and the way in which he prepared himself for performance. This quote captures his approach perfectly ...

You can't control whether you get good deliveries. Sometimes a ball comes along with your name on it and there's nothing you can do about it. But you can control your mental approach and how you approach every innings.[6]

Graham Thorpe, former England cricketer

So when you're getting ready to perform in a 'critical moment', the basis of your preparation should be rooted in identifying what your controllables are. Take a really close look at the situation and figure out exactly what you can, and cannot, control. It's worth writing these things down. My daughter Alexa, recently completed her Grade 4 piano examination. She was understandably anxious about the experience and was worrying about which scales the examiner would ask her to play, whether the keys on the exam piano would feel the same as ours at home, and how 'nice' the examiner was going to be. As we talked these concerns through, it became clearer to her that she could not control what the examiner was like or what she asked her to do. Neither could she control the feel of the piano keys. There were quite a few things that she could control, however. We decided on three – (1) take a few deep breaths before walking into the exam room so as to calm down, (2) slow down and play the set pieces at a steady pace, (3) enjoy the experience. I explained that this is exactly what elite athletes do when they prepare for a critical moment experience. They identify a few key 'controllables' and then focus entirely on them.

The somewhat eccentric, and often quoted baseball player of the 1970s and 1980s, Mickey Rivers, summed up control the controllables thinking with his famous quote …

> *Ain't no sense worrying about things you got no control over, 'cause if you got no control over them ain't no sense in worrying. And ain't no sense worrying about things you got control over, 'cause if you got control over them, ain't no sense worrying.*

Mickey Rivers, former basketball player

Have a 'process focus'

The quotes by Lawrence Dallagio, Alex Coomber and Graham Thorpe are all referring to the same thing in relation to controlling the controllables. They are referring to having a 'process focus'. These athletes know that they cannot ultimately control the outcome of events and so they restrict their focus to the processes inherent in the performance.

Compare the quotes by Petter Solberg and Ernie Els – two athletes from opposite ends of the sporting spectrum.

> *I've been so focused on what I can do and not on the championship because anything can happen.*[7]

Petter Solberg, after winning the Rally Drivers' World Championship in 2003

A rally driver performs on the edge all of the time. Taking a corner at 100mph with a line of trees a few centimetres from the side of the car requires the ultimate in nerve and composure. The slightest mistake can result in not only your own death but that of the co-driver as well.

> *I work on staying within myself and concentrating on what I have to do at any one moment. You are bound to get ahead of yourself at times. You must try not to. You must play each shot as well as you can and move on to the next one.*[8]

Ernie Els, South African golfer

A golfer, on the other hand, is performing in an environment with a very slow pace. You are 'thinking' for far longer than you are 'playing' in a typical round of golf. And yet, these two athletes are describing the same thing – having a process focus. In other words, thinking in the present and focusing on controllable processes that will impact positively on performance.

Let me introduce you to a simple framework used by athletes but about which I have had much positive feedback in my business consulting. It is a goal focusing framework which distinguishes between *outcome, performance* and *process* goals. Outcome goals relate to beating the opposition. Performance goals refer to the numbers (in sport that is points, times or distances; in business it could be targets for turnover, sales, waste reduction, staff retention rates etc.) required to achieve the outcome. Process goals are the controllable behaviours you need to engage in to deliver the performance goals. This could include tactics and strategy processes as well as attitude and thinking processes.

The table below illustrates examples from sport and business.

GOAL TYPE	SPORT (Long Jumper)	BUSINESS (Junior Sales Executive)
OUTCOME GOAL *The WHY*	Win Gold Medal at the National Championships	Win National Sales Award
PERFORMANCE GOAL *The WHAT*	Jump 8.25m in the Finals	Improve my sales by 8% from last year
PROCESS GOALS *The HOW*	Drive with arms in run-up High knee lift Reach long in jump	Get to sales meetings 10 minutes earlier to allow more time to prepare Ask more questions in the first 5 minutes of the meetings Maintain more eye contact during client conversations

I have used this simple framework successfully with business leaders who are putting annual business plans together and the principles within the structure can easily apply to organizational goal setting. However, for the purposes of this book, I shall focus on the individual. The example of an elite long jumper illustrates how the system works. First, we identify the *outcome* goal which in this case is to win the Gold Medal at the National Championships. This is an incredibly challenging goal and although realistic it does not tell us 'what' we need to do to achieve that dream goal. So, we do some analysis and figure out that a jump of 8.25 metres will be enough to beat the rest. We now have a *performance* goal which we have figured out by examining previous results, current form of the opposition and our own capabilities. Focusing on 8.25 metres immediately becomes a more specific target – and a more controllable one. However, we need to go one stage further. 'How' are we going to jump 8.25 metres? Working with our coach we now focus on three 'processes' which are entirely within our personal control and which, if executed correctly, will give us the best possible chance of landing the 8.25 metre jump. When getting ready to perform in the 'critical moment' where should our focus be? Not on winning the Gold Medal (despite it being the reason for us being there!). Nor on the actual 8.25 metres. We should be focused on our *process* goals – i.e. the three control-lable processes that we know will impact on our performance. These processes give us confidence and help us to avoid getting carried away with the intensity and pressure of the moment. It's sort of like 'going back to basics'. Get the basic performance processes right and the outcome will look after itself.

I tried not to think about the outcome and to concentrate on the performance.[9]
Nicola Benedetti, 16-year-old violinist, after winning the BBC's Young Musician of the Year

So for our junior sales executive who is desperate to win the national sales award (and secure the fantastic holiday which is on offer as an incentive!), he or she needs to do the analysis and figure out exactly what kind of numbers will need to be delivered to win the award – above and beyond the annual improvement target which will be imposed by the company anyway. Getting together with their boss or the National Sales Manager might be necessary to ascertain exactly what an appropriate extra target might be. In the example cited it is 8%. Then it is a case of identifying the controllable processes which need to be focused on during the critical performance moments – i.e. during sales meetings with customers. And it is those processes that should be focused on when the performance is taking place. As indicated in the table above, this individual needs to focus on arriving at sales meetings ten minutes earlier than usual so as to be better prepared, asking more questions in the first five minutes and maintaining more eye contact during conversations.

To broaden your thinking, the next table presents two further examples. These are merely presented to encourage you to always seek to work towards having real clarity around the key 'processes' in your performance – whether it be an individual, team or organizational performance. When performing in critical moments this is where your attention has to be – on the processes.

GOAL TYPE	HR middle manager	Retail Store Manager
OUTCOME GOAL *The WHY*	Get appointed to the senior manager position which is coming up in November	Win Regional Store of the month award
PERFORMANCE GOAL *The WHAT*	Improve my client evaluations by an average of 0.5 point	Increase 'like for like' sales by 4% Reduce waste by 11%
PROCESS GOALS *The HOW*	Respond to requests for information much quicker Spend 5 minutes extra preparing for client meetings Create a Confidence Peaks Chart and read it once per week for the next 3 months updating it as appropriate	Implement an extra 1–1 meeting with each of my top team Do an extra store walk per day and engage more with staff when doing so Devote two quality half days to coaching the warehouse team on the 3 new initiatives agreed last week

The Terry Francona quote illustrates the importance of maintaining a 'present focus' during critical performance moments and in my experience, the elite athletes that have a very clear knowledge of their 'process' goals are able to do this much better than those who lose the process focus.

> *I knew coming in what the expectations were from the outside. We just tried to stay in the moment. Even when things weren't going good.*[10]

Terry Francona, Coach to the Boston Red Sox when they famously won the World Series in 2004 for the first time in 86 years

When marathon record holder, Paula Radcliffe, was asked once about how she stays mentally tough her reply was related to having a 'process focus' although like many athletes she uses a little mind game to keep her attention in the here and now.

> *I count … I count to 100 three times – that's a mile. That's how I count the miles off. I think about the minute I'm in now rather than what's left to come.*[11]

Paula Radcliffe, after winning the 2003 London Marathon in world record time

England's Ashes 2005 goals approach
In his book, *Ashes Regained: The Coach's Story*, Duncan Fletcher outlines the approach to goal focusing which I had introduced to him prior to a previous tour of the West Indies and which

provides an illustration of the *outcome, performance, process* structure as it related to the Ashes summer of 2005.

> *We always determine our goals by the use of a definitive structure, a series of building blocks divided into three main processes: the why, the what and the how ... the why is the outcome goal ... the what is the performance goals in four disciplines: batting, bowling, fielding and the mental aspect of the game. Thus with batting, it was our goal to make at least 400 in the first innings of each Test in no more than 130 overs (we did that three times against Australia – they did not do it once) ... The how is obviously the actual procedure; the physical actions which need to take place for all this to come together. We emphasize key words such as concentration, communication and confidence in respect of this, but a common thread is to ensure that we replicate match conditions as closely as we can in practice. It is important to realize that each individual then has to undergo the same process, using the same structure (the why, the what and the how) in order to determine their own personal goals. That is entirely self-motivated. Each player is then given a sheet on which they lay out their own goals. They then hand that back to me before the First Test of the summer.*[12]

**Duncan Fletcher, Coach of the 2005 Ashes
winning England Cricket Team**

The table on the next page presents a blank version of the type of Goal Chart to which I introduced Duncan Fletcher.

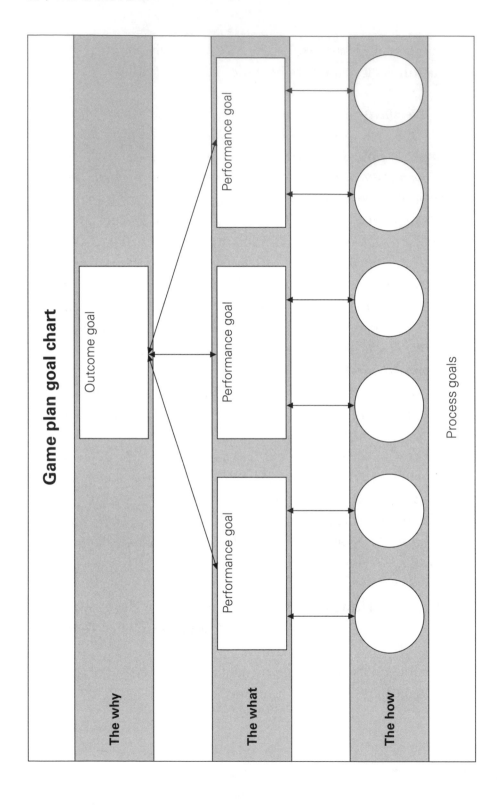

Game plan goal chart

In this blank version, you'll see that there are three boxes for the performance goals. This is not unusual as it is commonplace for people to focus on more than one area of the performance as being important in contributing to the outcome. As Fletcher himself pointed out, the England cricket team had four – one each for batting, bowling, fielding and the mental game. Likewise there are multiple boxes for the process goals. You'll need to adapt this chart to meet your own personal circumstances by merely choosing how many boxes you think you need at each of the three levels. As I keep pointing out, ultimately, what you're looking for is something that will assist you in focusing on the processes involved in your performance.

I have previously mentioned how Ashley Giles experienced a very difficult period of time after the defeat in the First Ashes Test match at Lord's and how reconnecting with his previous accomplishments helped him get back in the groove. He also did some work on refocusing on his processes prior to the Second Test at Edgbaston and made absolutely sure that when he stepped onto the field of play that's all he was thinking about. Since that time, when we are chatting informally over a coffee I will often ask him the question – 'How are your processes Gilo?'. He knows exactly what I mean and that the question is simply a reminder to be mentally tough by *controlling the controllables through having a process focus*.

TIP 5: SEE AND THINK SUCCESS

*Visualization. It has been called 'going to the movies'
and it may be the most important part of your mental
package.*[13]

**Ray Floyd, past winner of the PGA and US Open
golf tournaments**

*Negative thoughts lead to a negative performance; the
connection is as straightforward as that.*[14]

**Sally Gunnell, former Olympic Gold Medallist
and World Champion hurdler**

This tip is all about two fundamental psychological skills that all
(and I do mean *all*) top athletes use in some form or another.
I'm talking about visualization and self-talk. Many performers
refer to them as the building blocks to success. Visualization
refers to the pictures you have in your mind as you approach
a performance situation as indicated by the quote from Ray
Floyd. Self-talk describes the internal dialogue you have with
yourself – the importance of which is highlighted by Sally Gunnell. The classic example of both these elements in action is the
weekend golfer faced with a simple wedge to the green. Earlier
in the round they have played this shot beautifully but on the
16th hole the player is required to make exactly the same shot,
with exactly the same club, with only one difference – there
is a water hazard in front of the green. 'Don't lift your head'
they say to themselves. 'Don't go in the water. Don't do what
you did last week', they exhort internally as they address the
ball. Suddenly a clear picture appears in their mind of the ball
being horribly miss-hit and bobbling its way into the water. The
result? Surprise, surprise – head up, a topped shot and the ball

squirts into the hazard! The accomplished golfer on the other hand visualizes success and uses positive self-talk when faced with the same shot. 'Head still, swing slow, middle of the green' might be the words and the picture would definitely be of the ball sailing majestically into the target area. The now famous Jack Nicklaus quote drives this point home.

> *I never hit a shot even in practice without having a very sharp, in-focus picture of it in my head. It's like a colour movie. First I 'see' the ball where I want to finish. Then the scene quickly changes and I 'see' the ball going there. Then there's a sort of fade-out, and the next scene shows me making the kind of swing that will turn the previous images into reality.*[15]

Jack Nicklaus, golfing legend

We all engage in visualization and self-talk. They are everyday habits. The challenge is making them work for you – rather than against you. And this is a significant part of Critical Moment Toughness – using visualization and self-talk in a *facilitative*, rather than *debilitative*, manner. Consider for a moment what sort of visualization and self-talk you engage in immediately prior to a critical moment performance. Do you ever see yourself screwing up and making a hash of it? Do you ever imagine it all going wrong and you being left to dissect all the errors you made? Do you ever hear yourself saying things like 'I hope I don't blow it' or 'I hope I do a better job this time than the last time I was in this situation.'

I tend to rely on the visualization techniques that psychologist Steve Bull has introduced to the England players. Remembering a good innings, or even just a very good shot you've played, just before you go out to bat helps you to focus the mind and get rid of nerves.[16]

Nasser Hussain, former England Cricket Team captain

These are debilitating thoughts and absolutely will *not* help you demonstrate the mental toughness you'll need to deal with the demands of any critical moment performance. You simply *must* visualize success and think positively.

Morgan's apple juice

Of course, often our environment doesn't help us develop this positively focused thinking. Consider this vignette concerning my younger daughter Morgan. At an early age, Morgan developed a taste for apple juice and when she was about four years old was able to serve herself in the kitchen. Imagine the scene as she goes to the fridge to get the box of juice. She then goes to a cupboard, reaches up, and carefully takes out a cup. With total concentration, she then proceeds to pour the juice into the cup making sure that not a drop is spilled on the kitchen counter. Mission accomplished, she then puts the box of juice back in the fridge, collects her cup and starts to walk from the kitchen into the dining room. Imagine how she is feeling as she reflects on her competence. Without any help, she has made herself a drink and her confidence is riding high. Mum or Dad then walk into the room and what is the first thing we say? 'Don't spill that drink Morgan!' Immediately she experiences a reversal of emotion. In the space of a few seconds she goes from feeling competent and confident to worrying about the prospects of dropping the cup or causing a major spillage. Her now anxious mind creates a physical clumsiness resulting in her tripping and dropping the cup! It's like the old 'pink gorilla' thing. If I ask you right now to *not* think about a pink gorilla ... chances are that the first thing to enter your mind was exactly that – a pink gorilla! Our minds seem unable to program '*don't*' instructions and yet this is exactly

> *The greater our fear of making a mistake, the greater the likelihood that we will make a mistake.*[17]
>
> Sven-Goran Eriksson, former England football team coach

what we receive from parents, teachers, coaches and managers all through our lives.

Don't focus on don't!!

Laurie Graham was a Canadian downhill skier who competed in three Winter Olympics, won six World Cup races and was the first North American woman to win a World Cup Super Giant Slalom event. She presents a powerful description of how some of her coaches tended to focus on the 'don'ts' during race preparation time.

> *I don't like to think about don'ts before a race, like 'Don't do this or don't go too straight'. Instead of saying that, you say 'Stay on line and go with the flow'. We often corrected our coaches on that. We really found that don'ts came in as a negative. If, when we first inspected the course, the coach said, 'Don't come in here too straight or this will happen', then we were going through it in our mind; we'd remember more what we were not supposed to do. Now we just try and start positive right from the beginning. 'When you come in here, make sure you are high and come round the corner from behind.'* [18]

> **Laurie Graham, three times**
> **Olympic Canadian skier**

I recall several years ago now, recounting the Laurie Graham story to Bob Cottam who was bowling coach to the England Cricket Team for several years. Bob was an incredibly experienced coach who had worked at every level of the game over the previous 20 years. He listened to the story and then made the observation that so many cricket coaches wait at the locker room door and impart final words of wisdom as the players run out onto the field. He began to reflect on how frequently those final words were 'negatively orientated'. Statement such as 'no misfields today guys' or 'don't let them win the first half hour'. He went on to give further examples such as 'no wides today bowlers'. It was an astute observation by Bob and he vowed to be on the look out for it when he ran coaching clinics in the future.

Positive visualization examples in different walks of life

Every chef uses visualization. You have to visualize what you're going to put on the plate before you do it. I visualize the completed thing, then work back mentally, thinking and visualizing textures and contrasts ... I cook from noon to 3pm and from 7 to 11pm, and it's usually then, at the height of things, that I visualize, and create the best dishes.[19]

Gordon Ramsay, celebrity chef

When you do The Knowledge they tell you that one day you'll wake up and see the streets in your head. The Knowledge is all about visualization. I used to drive around on a bike with a clipboard on the front. When I got home I'd sit in a room and go over the runs that I'd done. I'd visualize the streets in my head, seeing all the landmarks and the cars parked on the roadside to get a real picture. It's no good just going over the run with a map; you want a picture of what you'll see when you're really doing the route.[20]

Garry Slattery, London cab driver

Visualizing myself in the Commons giving my maiden speech made me so nervous that I sat down at my PC and began shaking. Every time I visualized standing up in the chamber my heart started racing. But I visualized the whole thing through, including my movements and gestures; I'm sure that made it better. The best speeches are those where the speaker is visualizing something powerful as they talk.[21]

Lembit Opik, Liberal Democrat MP

When you put a needle into a vein, often you can't see it. You have the markings that you have been taught in anatomy, but you have to visualize beyond that. With an abdominal problem you have to envisage what the abdomen and the ruptured cells look like. It's very important when you're doing a procedure like an endoscopy.[22]

Dr Kevin Gunning, Consultant anaesthetist

So what should you do?

Simple. You do two things. First, make sure you observe you own self-talk and catch yourself when you start to use 'don't' or 'I can't' or 'I'm worried about' at the start of sentences. Second, make use of positive visualization as a preparation tool for critical moment performances. And if you think visualization is just for athletes look at the four quotes in the box below from a chef, a cab driver, a politician and an anaesthetist.

There must be ways in which you can utilize positive visualization as part of your Critical Moment Toughness game plan. Review the table on the next page for an overview of how visualization could be used for the 'clutch' situations described earlier in the book and then apply the principles to some of your own performance challenges.

Situation	Game Plan
One chance to clinch the big sales deal when the customer has lost interest	Visualize yourself conducting the meeting with confidence and articulating your 'pitch' in a clear, concise and coherent manner
Conducting a difficult 1–1 appraisal meeting when the other person is set on catching you out	Visualize yourself staying calm and focused. See yourself sticking to the agenda and remaining confident even when the conversation gets a little tricky
Making an important presentation in front of a large audience	Visualize the presentation going really well. Imagine your movements as well as your words. See yourself exuding confidence and speaking with clarity and conviction. Imagine yourself 'enjoying' the experience
Bumping into the CEO in the elevator and having a two minute opportunity to impress	If this is a realistic possibility and you want to make the most of it, then do some mental rehearsal in advance. Create the situation in your mind and play it through over and over so that when the opportunity presents itself you're ready to speak calmly and hence come across as confident and articulate rather than being caught off your guard
Performing in a job interview for a position in a company you have always wanted to work for and knowing this is your one big chance	Plan your interview strategy first and then mentally rehearse it relentlessly. See, and hear, yourself being fluent and confident. Think about the questions they may ask and visualize yourself responding with conviction. In particular mentally rehearse the kind of question that you are really concerned about. Prepare your response and practise it in your mind over and over again.

A final thought – move slow and breathe deep

One last thing to keep in mind when formulating your game plan for a critical moment performance is to be mindful of the physical aspects of your performance. Namely, your speed of movement and your breathing. Most people when they are under pressure tend to move quicker than normal and experience an elevation in breathing rate. Both these physical manifestations are *not* conducive to developing Critical Moment Toughness. Elite performers consciously slow their movements down and often use deep breathing as a calming strategy. The quotes by David Beckham and Nasser Hussain illustrate these points clearly.

I looked down at the ball before running up. It all went quiet. Everything was swirling around me, every nerve standing on edge. What's going on here? I can't breathe … I remember forcing in two big gulps of air to try and steady myself and take control.[23]

David Beckham, England and Real Madrid

Scyld Berry is a cricket writer I admire both as a journalist and as a friend because of my time writing with him for the Sunday Telegraph. Scyld has always got a theory about the game, quite often coming in from left field; but he really cares about the game and its players and he is quite an original, modern thinker. I was killing time in a coffee shop somewhere with Mike Atherton, as you do in Pakistan, and Scyld came up to us with his latest theory. 'I've been watching you two,' he said. 'Athers, perhaps because of his bad back, walked up to the table slowly. His heartbeat is low, his body language is calm and he seems relaxed. You Nass, are like a bundle of energy. You whisked up to the table. It was like, "What do I do next?" Why don't you just calm down, and get your heartbeat down?' At the time I was like 'Piss off, Scyld. What are you talking about? Low heartbeat and stuff? That's really going to help me against Wasim Akram!' But the more I thought about it, the more I felt he had a point.[24]

Nasser Hussain, former England Cricket Team captain

So I'm suggesting that you try to consciously slow your movements and general demeanour. Speak more slowly and deliberately. Be more graceful in the way you conduct yourself. You may be surprised at how this impacts on your sense of control and confidence. It may even help you to identify a good role model to help with this – someone who you admire for their physical presence and the way in which they speak with authority. Consider which bits you could emulate and how you could learn from the way they conduct themselves in challenging situations.

Consider also how you could utilize deep breathing better as a calming strategy. It only takes a few seconds but it can work wonders. In my experience, the most successful athletes work on their breathing as part of their preparation. They practise doing it regularly so that it comes easily when they are in the pressure situation. You can do the same in your performance world – remember, you're an athlete in your performance environment!

The Game Plan for Critical Moment Toughness

- Spend some time reflecting on how good you are generally at using 'control the controllables' thinking.

- Identify at least three situations coming up in the next month where you will need to focus on controlling the controllables.

- When faced with a critical moment situation in the future ask yourself the following questions:

1 What are the things that I can really have some control over in this performance situation?

2 What are the things that I must avoid worrying about because they are out of my control?

3 How am I going to ensure that I stay focused on the 'controllables'?

- Devise a simple goal framework which will help you identify your key 'processes' for any given 'critical moment' performance challenge – make sure you then take this 'process focus' into the performance situation.

- Identify when you demonstrate the tendency to use 'don't' when thinking about a performance challenge. Decide how you can focus on what you want to achieve as opposed to want you don't want to happen.

- Use visualization to prepare for any performance challenge but especially when Critical Moment Toughness is required. See yourself performing successfully and meeting the demands of the situation.

- Remind yourself to physically slow down immediately before a performance and take a few deep breaths if you need to calm yourself.

Endurance Toughness

If you can keep yourself physically fit and mentally alert, and have time to relax, then you will perform far better than people who work every minute of the day and never manage to break away from work.[1]

Sir Richard Branson, Chairman of the Virgin Group of Companies

This chapter is different. It is most definitely about resilience, which is at the heart of my mental toughness model, but it is not just about mental resilience. I'd like you to start thinking about physical resilience now as well. Staying healthy and physically robust is just another requirement of the modern day executive. If you can't do this then it is unlikely that you will be able to sustain periods of mental toughness for very long. I'm not talking here about 'athletic' physical robustness – i.e. making crunching tackles on a football field, lifting heavy weights in the gym or running marathons. I am referring to a much broader and more general type of physical health. One that allows you to meet the physical demands of modern corporate life in a way that enables the maintenance of clear thinking, good decision making and high performance. If you are tired, run down, or emotionally exhausted, sooner or later, your mental focus will be affected and inevitably your performance will drop. It is simply impossible to dispute this. People make poor decisions when they are tired. People make errors when they are under the weather. And people deliver suboptimal performance when they are expending too many resources on coping with the physical demands of their work environment.

Living in an age of stress

In the 1990s the World Health Organization began referring to stress as 'a worldwide epidemic'. It has been estimated that 40–50 million working days per year are lost to stress in the UK costing businesses literally billions of pounds. One in five employees admit to taking time off work due to stress and in 2004 the British Government published figures showing a 45% increase since 1997 in people being unable to work due to emotional problems. The information technology age has added huge pressure to our working lives creating a culture where people are expected to respond rapidly to any form of communication. Interruptions by email, phone and text are a constant challenge for most of us, as is the expectation to conduct business meetings over breakfast, lunch and dinner in addition to a regular working day. The world is shrinking and the inevitable consequence of a global economy is the need for people to travel more and more. Popping across the Atlantic for a day or two of work is commonplace now and the availability of internet access in airport lounges and hotels creates even more pressure to keep on top of things back in the office.

Innovations in technology and personal communications have, as Winston Fletcher pointed out in his book *Beating the 24/7* been both a blessing and a curse. Fletcher maintains that new ways of sending messages have added to the torrent of information with which managers must cope and have exponentially extended the possibilities for 'continual and unremitting communication'.

We have all seen the 'stressed' looking manager speaking passionately on their phone whilst speeding down the motorway knowing that they are late for a meeting. We have all experienced the booming voice in the airport terminal as someone finalizes a deal seconds before they board a plane. I was recently taking a weekend break in Venice and for an entire 30 minute boat ride, along with about 50 other passengers, I was subjected to a businessman who, although clearly on holiday, was shouting into his cell phone at a colleague about issues which were clearly of utmost importance to him and his company but of no interest to the rest of us whatsoever.

All this pressure and tension is exhausting to most people – both physically and mentally, but some appear to cope much better than others.

Cal Ripken Jr. played 17 seasons of major league baseball without ever taking a day off. This is, by all accounts, a monumental achievement and involved playing 2632 consecutive games in a sport known for its calendar of relentless grind. Games finish late at night and the team plane to the next venue arrives in the early hours. Injuries have little time to heal as teams play six days a week for six months in a season – 162 games in all. When Ripken broke the existing record, held by Lou Gehrig the legendary New York Yankee, he received a deafening ovation lasting 22 minutes from the crowd. People were awestruck by this athlete's incredible resilience, endurance and mental toughness. How did he do it? We'll probably never know for sure, but one thing that is clear relates to the way in which Ripken 'looked after' his body and stayed in good physical shape. He was a player ahead of his time in this regard, and reaped the benefits throughout his astonishing 17 year career record. The quote from Michael Atherton posits the theory that there is a link between physical fitness and mental toughness for athletes. What might the equivalent be in corporate life?

> *All I can say is that when I was at my most toughest I was also at my fittest and when I felt least tough I was at my least fittest. So the combination of the two leads me to believe there is a big link. My feeling is that by being physically tough and fit that kind of gives you an in-built confidence which translates into help in the mental game.*[2]

Michael Atherton,
former England Cricket team captain

Let's revisit our IT specialist Paul who I described earlier in the book. He is travelling excessively in his effort to meet the demands of his current job situation. He is being dragged into more and more meetings and things are getting to be too much. His body is not coping well with the travel and both his performance, and health, are suffering. In short, Paul is probably not managing his energy as well as he could by failing to pay adequate attention to his lifestyle management. He needs a dose of Endurance Toughness. But this is absolutely not just a simple matter of telling him to toughen up, grit his teeth and stop being so weak. He needs some specific advice on what changes he can make to his lifestyle to give him the physical and mental strength to deal with the relentless demands he is currently facing. The two tips outlined in this section of the book should be compulsory reading for Paul.

TIP 6: MANAGE YOUR ENERGY

In recent years, performance psychologists have been focusing more and more on the impact of managing energy. In their book, *The Power of Full Engagement*, Jim Loehr and Tony Schwartz claim that 'managing energy, not time, is the fundamental currency of high performance'.[3] My experience of working with executives at all levels in organizations concurs with this. That is not to say that being skilful at time management is not important. Far from it. If you are unable to adequately manage all the different demands on your time and prioritize accordingly then you will not achieve your optimal performance. However, good time management is not necessarily the panacea for dealing with stress and pressure – particularly when it comes to mental toughness. Managing your energy is the key to unlocking your performance potential – especially in a corporate world that can be so relentless and exhausting. So how do we go about managing our energy? How do we look after our minds and bodies so that they can deal with the pressurized world of the 21st century business person? Before answering that question, let's briefly review some basic physiology to help us appreciate what is happening to us when we find ourselves succumbing to the debilitative effects of chronic stress.

Cortisol – the stress hormone!

Cortisol is a really important, and useful, hormone which is secreted by the adrenal glands. Our body produces it naturally with production being higher in the mornings to give us energy for the day. In the evenings, our cortisol levels drop by up to 90% as a result of us being more relaxed and winding down from the pressures of the day. At low levels, cortisol helps our body fight infection and heal damaged tissues after injury or illness. It gives us bursts of energy and can heighten our cognitive functioning. It is essential for our implementation of the fight-

or-flight response mechanism which helps us cope with acute stress by mobilizing our body's resources ready for action. However, our bodies do not respond well when our cortisol levels remain elevated for long periods of time and this is exactly what happens when we experience chronically busy and stressful lives. In ancient times, humans reacted quickly when placed in a stressful situation, which often involved a risk to their life from predators. On assessing the danger, their bodies secreted cortisol which mobilized their fight-or-flight response – they either stood there and fought, or ran away. Either way the external stress was removed following which the cortisol levels dissipated and some sort of equilibrium was re-established. The difference these days is that our stressors do not go away – rather, they are ever present in the form of long working hours, daily traffic jams, financial worries and job pressures. Consequently, our cortisol levels remain elevated for much longer periods of time. The medical research evidence now clearly demonstrates that sustained high levels of cortisol lead to all sorts of potentially harmful physiological changes – including blood sugar problems, fat accumulation, elevated blood pressure, heart problems, memory loss, thyroid issues and a general decrease in the efficiency of the body's immune function. At best, these changes will compromise our capacity to think clearly and demonstrate resilience. At worst they will lead to illness and disease. The fundamental issue here is that our bodies cope really well with acute stress – i.e. anything short term. However, the problem arises when the stress becomes chronic – i.e. sustained over longer time periods. So, in summary, left unchecked, stress can wreak havoc on our health, by causing a susceptibility to illness, a loss of energy, and sometimes even increases in feelings of anxiety and depression.

Three manageable ways of reducing the impact of stress, moderating our cortisol levels and hence managing our energy more effectively are focused around (1) physical activity; (2) nutrition and (3) relaxation. Our IT specialist, Paul, would probably benefit from taking a close look at each in formulating a game plan for managing his energy more effectively.

Physical activity

The research into the beneficial effects of exercise and physical activity in mediating the stress response are well documented in the scientific literature. Indeed, some experts even go so far as to argue that nothing eases stress more than exercise. It's also quite strange to reflect that 'expending energy' in the short term (by exercising) is an effective way of 'boosting your energy' in the longer term and hence managing your overall energy levels. The positive effects of exercise are not only physical but also mental and a review of the available literature suggests that, among others, the following benefits exist:

- Lowering of cortisol levels.
- Increase in cardiovascular functioning by strengthening the heart muscles and increasing the elasticity of blood vessels.
- Reduction in bad cholesterol.
- Increase in levels of endorphins – those feel-good chemicals you read about that have a positive effect on mood.
- Improvements in concentration and memory.
- Improvements in sleep patterns.

Despite these incredibly powerful incentives for making exercise and physical activity part of your everyday life, the majority of people do not engage in anywhere near enough physical activity. The excuses vary – lack of time, lack of facilities, too tired, it's boring, it's painful, or simply can't be bothered. Well, if you really want to develop your all round mental toughness and hence acquire that 'winning edge', you must consider the role that physical activity will play as part of your game plan. I'm not necessarily talking here about joining a gym and attending fitness classes or training for the London Marathon. I am going to simply challenge you to think about how you can increase your physical activity in 'bite sized chunks' in the way that Sharon Stone suggests in the quote below when asked how she had managed to maintain such a fabulous figure at the age of 48 when she released the movie *Basic Instinct 2* in 2006.

> *I'd like to release an exercise video, as I'm bored of being asked how I keep myself in shape. It would be impractical to film though, as it's the simple things that work best: parking your car that extra block away from the store. Or taking the stairs rather than elevator.*[4]

Sharon Stone, movie actress

Sharon Stone's quote reflects a trend in exercise prescription that has been developing in recent years – namely a move away from the old-fashioned 'no pain no gain' approach of the 70s and 80s. Experts are nowadays much more inclined towards focusing on increasing levels of moderate activity as a means of promoting good health. Whilst this does not rule out the gym and serious jogging regimes for those that want it (and I would personally recommend these activities if you have the commitment), it means that you can still acquire significant health gains from activity without doing anything too formal. There's even a term that is now being used to describe this type of approach to physical activity – 'integrative exercise'. It is beginning to receive coverage within the mainstream media and Dr Harvey Simon, an associate professor of medicine at the Harvard Business School has stated: 'You can reap enormous health benefits with no sweat exercise … everything that gets you moving – from gardening to sex – can and will contribute to your health.'

He has even published a book on the subject called *The No Sweat Exercise Plan: Lose Weight, Get Healthy and Live Longer*.

Even the *Financial Times* published a feature article in its special report on The Global Traveller on 3 April, 2006.

> *'Many fitness experts maintain making time for daily exercise is just as important as scheduling meetings, transport and the rest ... And it should all help performance in business meetings. Pack an old pair of running shoes that you need not bring home. Take shorts and a T-shirt that you can wash in your bathroom. Above all, say experts, do no overdo the fitness regime. Remember that 20 minutes exercise is better than nothing.'*

> **Financial Times, 6.4.06**

So let's consider some ways in which you can 'manage your energy' better by being more active in small doses whilst not disrupting your day too much.

Idea 1: The stairs

Before tackling the issue of stairs, I am constantly amazed at how many people stand still on horizontal conveyors in airport terminals. They walk from one to the next and then upon setting foot on the moving belt they come to an abrupt halt. I am genuinely bemused by their attitude particularly if they have just got off a plane and their legs are crying out to be used. So here's a small start for some. Begin walking on these horizontal conveyors. Then I would suggest taking stairs rather than escalators and eventually you'll be ready to go for the big one – i.e. hotel or office block stairs rather than the elevator! You'll be astonished at how this simple act gets the heart rate going and burns calories. Imagine taking an extra 6 or 8 flights of stairs per day – perhaps around 50 extra per week. This simple act would impact significantly on your health and general well-being. Even if you're destination is the 17th floor, why not take the elevator to the 12th floor and walk the rest of the way? Try it – you'll be pleasantly surprised.

Idea 2: The car park

Actively look to park your vehicle in the car park some way from the office or hotel door – even if it's raining (just keep an umbrella in the car). The extra walk to and from the building will add another little piece of activity to your day. If you have a couple of bags to carry all the better as you get the benefits from some natural weight training as well.

Idea 3: Consider walking first

When you have a short journey to take – such as going into town or moving from one office to another within a short distance – consider walking as your first option rather than driving. It's amazing how far you'll find you can walk in just 20 minutes at a moderate pace (more than a mile for most people).

Idea 4: Lunchtime – a chance to be active

I am fully aware that taking time for lunch is frowned upon in some corporate cultures although I cannot understand why. Having a break and then refocusing later usually results in higher productivity for most people – our brains get tired as well as our bodies. My advice to the people I coach is to use lunchtime (even if you only have 20 minutes) as an opportunity for getting some fresh air and a brisk walk. It's another chance to get a 10 minute period of activity under your belt for the day.

Idea 5: Be creative

I travel a great deal in my job as a business consultant and sport psychologist. This involves staying in many different types of hotel – some of which are luxurious with state of the art gymnasia whilst others are not quite so elegant. I enjoy working out and am always frustrated when I check into a hotel and find that there is no gym. However, rather than get too dejected and frustrated that I shall not be able to get my workout, it is not unusual for me to spend a quick ten minutes running up and down the hotel stairs. I am absolutely not self-conscious about this as I am totally convinced of the merits of doing a short ten minute burst of exercise rather flopping into a chair and watching some TV that really doesn't interest me.

Idea 6: Double up

Why not combine short periods of exercise with doing something else – such as listening to the radio or watching a DVD? Some simple stretching exercises in front of the TV is an excellent way to kill two birds with one stone as they say. Spend ten minutes watching the news whilst doing a series of sit-ups, press-ups and a few minutes skipping. Alternatively spend some money on purchasing a piece of home exercise equipment and keep it in the spare bedroom. If it's a bicycle ergometer, why not sit on it and read the newspaper or a novel whilst pedalling away?

So why not consider how you could use these six ideas to generate a plan for grabbing the equivalent of two or three ten-minute 'informal' workouts per day. You may be surprised at how easy this becomes once you change your mindset and set some goals.

If you can integrate physical activity into your general lifestyle and commit to making it a priority, you will undoubtedly manage your energy more efficiently. Your immune system will be stronger and you will generally feel more energetic and healthier. All these benefits will combine to assist you in coping with the stresses involved in your everyday life and equip you with an increased dose of Endurance Toughness.

Nutrition

It's interesting that when we feel stressed and our cortisol levels are running high, we have a tendency to crave the kind of foods that will exacerbate, rather than ease, the problem. Consider your own eating patterns when you're feeling under pressure – do you tend to aim for things like biscuits, chips, crisps, sandwiches filled with mayonnaise, cakes, doughnuts, chocolate bars etc.? Most people do but unfortunately this will not help in managing our energy over the long term. This type of food tends to give us a quick 'burst' of energy but very soon afterwards our energy levels drop again significantly. They simply do not help and will not assist us in developing resilience, concentration and clear thinking when we have to perform during pressurized times.

Both Professor John Oxford, an expert in virology at the Royal London Hospital, and Professor Ron Eccles, Director of the Common Cold Centre at Cardiff University highlight the importance of maintaining a robust immune system for fighting off coughs, colds and flu and dietary considerations are very much a part of this process.

> *It is proven that if you have a very bad diet, you are much more susceptible to infections.*[5]

Professor Ron Eccles, Director of the Common Cold Centre at Cardiff University

There are a number of quite basic and easy to implement nutritional strategies, which will help give your immune system a boost and assist in managing your energy appropriately. The table opposite provides some very basic advice.

Immune system foods	Game plan advice
Live yoghurts. For some time now, research results have shown that yoghurts made with certain 'good' bacteria (called probiotics) are helpful in aiding digestion but more recent research suggests that they may also have a beneficial effect on the immune system	Consider eating probiotic yoghurt on breakfast cereal, as a mid-morning snack or as a desert with dinner
Fruit & veg. As you would expect, a well-balanced diet including plenty of fruit and vegetables, contributes hugely to immune system maintenance	Be as conscientious as you can about getting your 5–8 portions of fruit and vegetables each day. Consider adding fruit to your breakfast cereal or eating a portion as a snack during the day.
Vitamin C. No doubt you have read in recent years about the critical role that antioxidants play in the prevention of disease. One of the strongest antioxidants is vitamin C. Good sources of vitamin C are citrus fruits, green peppers, cantaloupes and broccoli. Vitamin C has also been shown to reduce the length of time it takes to recover from a cold	Monitor the ways in which you get Vitamin C into your diet and set a daily goal of eating something rich in it
Vitamin E. Another important antioxidant and has been shown to slow down the symptoms of aging as well as strengthening body cells that fight infection. Good sources are wholegrain foods and vegetable oils	Eat wholegrain bread rather than white and try to consume a regular portion of wholegrain cereal. Cook in vegetable oil rather than animal fat
Carotenoids. These are antioxidants that help to strengthen the immune system by producing lymphocytes. The best sources for carotenoids are the red, yellow and orange fruits and vegetables such as carrots, tomatoes and pumpkin as well as green leafy foods	Try aiming for a 'colourful' salad a few times per week. Make your own at home using tomatoes, peppers, carrots, spinach leaves and pumpkin seeds. Be creative in finding a concoction that suits your taste buds but don't expect this to be immediately appetising – you may have to stick with it for a while

Immune system foods	Game plan advice
Water. The health benefits of drinking plenty of water during the day are multi-faceted and well-documented. Some experts even claim that keeping well hydrated is one of the best ways of controlling elevated cortisol levels. When we get dehydrated, our performance suffers through decrease in concentration levels and focusing skills. Remember also, that caffeine is a diuretic and therefore contributes to dehydration.	Aim to drink between 1 and 2 litres of water each day. Carry a bottle in your briefcase and certainly keep one topped up on your office desk. Drink little and often and accept that if you wish to drink coffee or other caffeinated beverages then you will need to take on extra water to compensate. Reducing caffeine generally is a good bet anyway.

Part of your mental toughness game plan simply must involve making eating properly a priority. Food is your body's fuel and in addition to being mindful of the immune system benefits of quality nutrition, don't underestimate the basics which are always worth revisiting.

Here are three basics that should be easy for you to remember and implement:

1 Eat fresh rather than pre-packaged or processed foods as much as possible.

2 Ensure you consume high fibre foods on a daily basis.

3 Aim to reduce sugar, fat and calorie-laden food and drinks whenever you can – you don't need to cut them out completely, but moderation is crucial.

Snacking?

A very common mistake that people make is to eat the wrong things when they feel hungry in between meals. Most people reach for convenience foods which taste good at the time of eating and appear to give an immediate boost to energy levels. Things like a chocolate bar or biscuits. However, the effects are misleading and these food types actually undermine energy levels. This is due to their 'glycemic index' which is a measure of how fast a food raises blood sugar level. Essentially, foods that score high in glycemic index (or GI for short) will cause a quick buzz but then a dip will follow and energy levels will drop leading to a dip in mental alertness as well. If you're feeling peckish during the day and sense your energy levels dropping consider grabbing a handful of nuts, seeds and raisins rather than a quick bowl of chips or bag of crisps. In terms of setting yourself up for the day, the best type of cereals to eat at breakfast time are those with an oatmeal base. These will score low in GI and hence have a much longer lasting impact on your energy levels. Porridge is a really good one. Or if you haven't got time to prepare it warm, then sprinkle some plain oats into other cereals, add some fruit and nuts and make your own muesli.

Fred's advice to 'road warriors'

Dr Fred Wadsworth is the nutrition expert for the England Cricket Team. He works with each player helping them develop a nutrition plan that will improve their capacity to manage their energy levels over the course of a day's play and throughout a long overseas tour. I asked Fred if he could apply his knowledge and come up with some tips for those readers who have to deal with the road warrior syndrome – i.e. those who travel excessively as part of their job and are under pressure to stay connected, focused and alert during busy and stressful journeys to, and from, the workplace. Managing energy when you are away from home on business – particularly if you are having to deal with long journeys and overnight stays in hotels is a real challenge. Below are Fred's ten rules for managing energy on the road when you are unable to maintain your usual routines.

Ten road warrior rules for managing energy

1   Dehydration is common and often subtle but powerful in its effects. Generally aim for at least two litres of *water* every day. Drink water, not sweetened drinks. Keep alcohol to a minimum.

2   Eat regular meals and *never* miss breakfast. Overcome perceptions of pressure of time – eating is *essential* to performance. Jet lag may interfere with appetite but eat something at the right times of day to help establish a normal daily rhythm. Each meal should contain a good mix of protein, above-ground veg and unrefined carbohydrates (brown).

3   Keep your 'junk' food intake to a minimum – have them as a treat rather than instead of eating properly.

4   Avoid sweet and refined stuff to stop swinging blood sugar levels. This will support energy levels and concentration.

5   Think seriously about how you manage your fat intake. Travelling and lots of business dinners are often an excuse to be fat and unhealthy. Avoid saturated fats and starchy foods at night. Use hotels to your advantage, they will produce food to order so healthy choices need not be an aggravation. For example, eat porridge for breakfast rather than sugary cereal.

6   Eat enough protein. It will manage your appetite and helps keep hold of your muscle. An average sedentary adult needs at least two portions of protein a day.

7   Do some physical exercise; hotels have gyms, either use them or try the alternative suggestions outlined in this chapter! Exercise will help manage stress, improve sleep patterns and gut function. It will also help maintain general health.

8   Supplements can be helpful for some, particularly when travelling overseas. A decent multivitamin can be helpful if changes in diet are significant when you travel. Probiotics will help immunity, gut function and provide protection from traveller's diarrhoea.

9   Don't look for short cuts. Get in good habits and stick to them.

10   Get enough sleep. This is when you grow muscle. If you find you are waking at night to drink, then hydrate properly during the day. If you are waking to pass urine then stop fluid intake at 8pm.

Dr Fred Wadsworth, Nutrition Doctor for England Cricket Team, 2006

Fred can be contacted by email at fred@nutritiondoctors.co.uk so if you, or your company, is interested in pursuing the diet and nutrition element of mental toughness further, then why not contact him and discuss how he might help you?

So to conclude this section, on the basis of the advice presented, now consider what you can start doing tomorrow to improve your basic nutrition so that you are positively influencing your immune system and energy levels. Make this a priority and view it as a fundamental part of your game plan.

Relaxation

The effects of relaxation are well documented in the medical literature and it is not difficult to see why they contribute to the development of resilience and mental toughness. Effective relaxation therapies result in a lowering of blood pressure, reduction of muscle tension, decrease in heart rate, an increase in blood flow to the stomach, intestines and kidneys, and a decrease in blood sugar levels. These effects are brought about by the autonomic nervous system which is the regulatory structure in our body that helps people adapt to changes in their environment through the involuntary vital functions such as the digestive, circulation and adrenal systems. It helps regulate our blood pressure, the activity of our heart, the movement and work of our stomach, intestine and salivary glands as well as the secretion of insulin. The autonomic nervous system has two branches or subsystems – the sympathetic and the parasympathetic. The sympathetic branch kicks into gear when we are under stress and triggers reactions which will mobilize us for action. As described earlier, these are fine as long as they do not stick around too long and start to drain our energy and resources. To counterbalance the effects of the sympathetic branch of the autonomic nervous system, we need to trigger the parasympathetic branch. Essentially, this reverses the mobilizing effects, triggering what is referred to in the scientific literature as 'The Relaxation Response' – a term first described by Dr Herbert Benson from Harvard University in 1968. Our bodies, and minds, often crave to experience this type of relaxation without us even being aware of it until it is too late. Elite athletes work this out early in their careers and develop their own personal strategies for creating the relaxation response. Some favour a regular massage or attending yoga classes – both of which are extremely effective in inducing the relaxation response. Tai Chi or meditation programmes are favoured by others. Each has its merits in triggering the parasympathetic nervous system and countering the ill-effects of long term stress. Some recent research conducted by Professor Angela Clow from the Department of Psychology at the University of Westminster has even demonstrated that a 40 minute visit to an art gallery can trigger significant reduction in the cortisol levels of high flying business people! However, I'd like to focus here on a technique which I have taught to hundreds of athletes and business people. It combines deep breathing and an adapted form of a process called Progressive Muscle Relaxation. The table below describes the technique, which I call the '10/10 Relaxation Routine'. As you will see it has 10 steps and takes 10 minutes. You may find this quite easy to do straightaway but many people find it very difficult at first. Don't be put off if you struggle the first few times you attempt it. The process is a skill and as such the more you practise it the better you will become.

I normally challenge people to do this exercise as often as they can but at least three times per week as a minimum. Remember, it only takes ten minutes and even if this means closing your office door at some point in the working day I'd recommend it.

The 10/10 Deep Relaxation Routine
(Ten steps in ten minutes)

STEP 1: Find a place where you can sit down comfortably (preferably with your head supported) and where you will not be interrupted. Switch off your phone or pager so that no one can contact you for the next ten minutes.

STEP 2: Put on some music which you find really relaxing – a personal music player is a useful accessory.

STEP 3: Close your eyes and then spend a couple of minutes getting really comfortable and tuning into your body whilst switching off from the outside world.

STEP 4: Now focus on your breathing rhythm. Count ten deep breaths to establish a slow, steady breathing rhythm. Each time you breathe out, feel more relaxed and feel some tension drain away.

STEP 5: When you feel ready, focus on your right arm. Clench your fist tightly, hold while you count to five, and then slowly open out your fingers and relax your hand and arm completely. Feel your arm go heavy and sink into the floor or chair. Repeat this process for your left arm.

STEP 6: Now focus on your right leg. Tighten the muscles in your leg, hold while you count to five, and then relax all the muscles completely. Concentrate on a heavy feeling throughout the length of your leg. Repeat the process for your left leg.

STEP 7: Turn your attention to your face, neck and shoulders. Relax all the muscles in this area and in particular focus on smoothing out the muscles in your forehead. Relax your cheeks, your neck and the back of your shoulders.

STEP 8: Focus on relaxing your whole body by concentrating on a relaxed feeling in your fingertips, toes and forehead.

STEP 9: Spend a couple of minutes listening to your music, enjoying this relaxed feeling and imagining yourself in a place where you can feel completely relaxed and at ease. This may be on the beach, by a swimming pool, on a boat, in a forest, up a mountain, etc.

STEP 10: Count down silently, and slowly, from ten to one. As you do, bend and stretch your arms, move your head from side to side and gradually bring yourself back. As you get to number one, open your eyes and tell yourself that you feel relaxed, rested and refreshed.

Steve's story

Steve is a management consultant who I coached a few years ago. During our sessions, we covered lots of different areas relating to his work performance but we kept coming back to elements of his Endurance Toughness. Over the course of several months Steve created a game plan which contained aspects of physical activity and improved diet but he was really struggling to fit a relaxation slot into his busy schedule. It was not that he wasn't convinced of the benefits of the 10/10 Relaxation Routine but that he simply couldn't land a plan that worked for him. Eventually, knowing how many miles Steve did a year on business travel in his car, I advised him to consider the 'on the road' relaxation plan. Basically, I suggested that he practised using the 10/10 technique to break up a long car journey. The plan involved him keeping a CD of relaxation music permanently in the glove compartment of his car and a small cushion on the back seat. His goal then, at least three times per week, was to pull into a motorway service station, park the car in a corner somewhere and accept that he was out of work mode for the next ten minutes. He switched his phone off, locked the car doors, inserted the relaxing CD into the car's music system, reclined his seat whilst resting his head on the cushion, and conducted a 10/10 Relaxation Routine. By doing this, Steve was actually achieving two things at once. He was triggering his parasympathetic nervous system and receiving all the longer term health benefits resulting from a reduction in cortisol levels as well as following the recommended principle of taking a break from a long and often stressful drive, to combat 'road warrior fatigue' and the associated dangers of driving when tired. This was a manageable plan for Steve and he still sticks to it to this day claiming that it is a vital part of his mental toughness game plan. So when you next see an executive car parked in the far corner of a motorway services car park containing what looks like a sleeping middle-aged business man reclined in the driver's seat, he's not sleeping. He's midway through a 10/10 Relaxation Routine which is providing his body and mind with a valuable energy boost.

Another added benefit of practising the 10/10 Relaxation Routine regularly and hence getting more and more proficient at reaching a deep state of relaxation is that you will find yourself better able to implement the short version which I refer to as the 'three step quick-fire relaxation trick'. The table BELOW outlines how to do this. It's a great little technique which is pinched from what many elite athletes do immediately before they perform. As you'll notice, it's closely aligned to the 'move slow and breathe deep' technique that I introduced you to when concluding the Critical Moment Toughness section of the book. I'd now encourage you to consider when you might use this technique as a way of staying calm in situations that would normally raise your blood pressure. Here are some examples:

- When the person at the check-in desk is not being co-operative and you can feel yourself getting agitated and annoyed.
- When the passenger sitting across from you is being rude and irritating.
- When your colleague says something that really gets on your nerves and your normal tendency would be to snap back and then regret it later.
- As a parent, when your child asks you for something at the worst possible moment and seems completely oblivious to your own life challenges.
- When your boss is unjustly critical of something you have done and you feel enraged at their comments.
- When you get a puncture at the one time in the year you would choose for it not to happen.

- When you run for 20 minutes to catch a train only to see it pulling away as you arrive on the platform.
- When the printer in your office at home malfunctions at a critical time and you cannot think of how to get around this major catastrophe!

As you can appreciate, this list could go on and on and on. In fact, why don't you pause – right now – for a couple of minutes and write down your own personalized list of irritating and stress-inducing events? Think of situations in which you are aware of your physiological response and the stress hormones flying around your body. Visualize how you might counter that awful 'stressed' feeling by using the 'three step quick-fire trick'. It's a skill remember though, and you'll get better and better the more you practise it – just like the elite athletes.

The three step quick-fire relaxation trick

STEP 1: Either sitting or standing, remain still and focus on calming your body and mind. It helps to try to relax your fingertips and your toes.

STEP 2: Breathe deeply in through the nose and out through the mouth according to the following routine:

Inhale through nose: Count IN, TWO, THREE, FOUR.

Exhale through mouth: Count OUT, TWO, THREE, FOUR.

(Repeat if necessary and time permits.)

STEP 3: Before re-focusing on the outside world, repeat silently a phrase such as 'I feel calm' or 'I know I can cope'.

So that's the end of 'Tip 6 – Manage your Energy'. Mentally tough performers are able to endure the challenges of the road warrior factor – looking after themselves by managing the three key aspects of their lifestyle – (1) their physical activity levels, (2) their nutrition, and (3) their ability to relax.

> *You need discipline in your lifestyle, because that affects anybody's achievement factor. Show me somebody who's not tight in the disciplines of living, and I'll show you somebody who hasn't reached the limit of their true potential.*[6]

> **Jackie Stewart, former World Champion**
> **Formula 1 Driver**

TIP 7: MANAGE YOUR OUTLOOK

> *When you are 2–1 up against Australia and on the verge of something special, you don't seem to feel tired; your body doesn't ache.*[7]

> **Andrew Flintoff, reflecting on the final match in**
> **the 2005 Ashes series**

Andrew Flintoff's quote reminds us how our state of mind can have a positive influence on our body. In early September of 2005, he and his fellow team-mates were coming to the end of the most pressurized period of their careers. They were experiencing considerable mental and physical fatigue, not to mention that some were carrying niggling injuries. Their bodies had given everything for the entire summer and their minds had had to endure amazing levels of intensity and pressure. They had made critical decisions at critical times. They had delivered world class performances in 'clutch' situations. They had absorbed the excitement and adulation of the nation in their quest to achieve what had eluded them for the previous 18 years. They were ready for a well-deserved break but there was one more match to play – the big one. The match that would ultimately result in them becoming legends of the game through their glorious series victory and a trip to Buckingham Palace to receive their OBEs and MBEs. Apparently, the Queen even told Michael Vaughan that she watched the series avidly but that it all got a bit tense for her and was a bit 'nerve-wracking'. Going into this final match, though, the players needed to demonstrate Endurance Toughness. Just as they had to again at the end of the winter tour to India the following year. This was a tour that was plagued by setback after setback. Touring the sub-continent is a massive challenge at the best of times, as the quote from Derek Pringle points out. But when things start to go wrong it becomes a long, and arduous battle, which requires immense levels of Endurance Toughness.

> *Precious is the player who can still do a job with a throat sandpapered by dust and pollution and when the lower abdomen has just performed its fourth somersault of the day.*[8]

Derek Pringle, former England cricketer and
***Daily Telegraph* correspondent**

England ended up playing this series without four (and five for the last match) of their Ashes winning side. Flintoff was thrown in at the deep end and required to captain the side in the absence of both captain Vaughan and vice-captain Trescothick. In historic fashion, the team managed to draw the series 1–1 by winning a match on Indian soil for the first time in 21 years. The series had been a relentless battle played out in scorching temperatures under the most challenging circumstances. Fitness, nutrition and relaxation all played a part but the way in which the players went about 'managing their outlook' was also a significant contribution to the end result. In communication I had with the players and coaching staff during that series, I distinctly recall them commenting on how good the spirit was among the team. They were steadfastly refusing to be dragged down by all the unfortunate events of the tour and were remaining positive and upbeat about their chances of performing against all the odds. The contribution of this positive mental approach during adversity cannot be underestimated in terms of its impact on performance and makes a perfect introduction to 'Tip 7: Manage your outlook'. Like managing your energy, I'm going to cover three basic facets of managing your outlook which are, (1) optimism, (2) highlights and (3) perspective. Let's look at each in turn.

Optimism

Professor Martin Seligman, from the University of Pennsylvania, is a world-renowned authority on positive psychology and has published a wealth of material on the subject. In his work, he discusses the steady flow of scientific evidence that is now available to show that having an 'optimistic' outlook on life has demonstrable effects – not only on how

If you've got a good attitude, you're positive and you work at your game, you can do what you like.[9]
Duncan Fletcher, Coach of 2005 Ashes winning England Cricket Team

people deal with setbacks, but on how it improves general mood and boosts the immune system. People with an optimistic outlook on life tend to be more motivated, persevere at challenges longer and, not surprisingly, are more successful in the long term. Optimism is an essential attitude for developing Endurance Toughness and yet, as we know, so many people demonstrate a pessimistic outlook which often drags those around them, as well as themselves, in a downward spiral of negativity. I sometimes use the term 'negaholic' to describe the attitude of these individuals. You know the type. Whatever, the situation they will find something wrong with it. They constantly point out the flaws in new ideas. They see catastrophe in every event, are cynical, blame others and are generally a massive energy drain on those around them. Contrast this with someone who seems to possess 'dispositional optimism'. They are happy, look to find positives in all situations, bring energy to a team and generally are good to be around on account of their enviable outlook on life. Although people have a natural tendency to go one way or the other on the optimism–pessimism scale, Professor Seligman claims, and indeed demonstrates, that you can 'learn' to be more optimistic. In fact, his book *Learned Optimism: How to change your mind and your life* presents a compelling case for exactly this.

When you turn up at the ground midway through a game it should be impossible to tell from the attitude of the fielding team whether they are on top or behind. You should have to look on the scoreboard, not see it on the field.[10]
Shane Warne,
Australian cricketer
who was voted one of
the five Wisden players
of the century in 2000

The philosophy behind encouraging a more optimistic approach to challenge is not rooted in the belief that everyone must be blissfully happy and completely optimistic all of the time in every single situation that is encountered. Cynics and pessimists do sometimes play a valuable role in teams by maintaining the necessary reality checks which can get lost in an overly excitable optimistic approach to life. Nevertheless, when the challenge is dealing with relentless pressure and stress, then the evidence is absolutely clear … find the positives and be optimistic. This is exactly what the England Cricket Team had to do in India in February and March of 2006.

Their side was depleted. The climate was harsh and unfamiliar to most of the squad. They were fielding three rookie players and it was the end of an extremely difficult winter involving a tour to Pakistan as well as India. The players were tired and keen to return home to partners and families. An optimistic outlook was essential and, led by the stand-in captain Andrew Flintoff, the team displayed immense Endurance Toughness by keeping hold of a strong belief that they would perform well and achieve their goals.

Challenge your own disposition

Most of us get drawn into the pessimistic thinking style from time to time and this is natural. However, developing your mental toughness is about challenging yourself when you feel this happening. You must take control of your mind and 'think differently'. Consider the quote from Darren Clarke which reinforces this point, and indeed the many years of research and scholarship conducted by Professor Martin Seligman and his colleagues – namely, that your attitude can shape the experiences you have in life, and ultimately, how successful you are.

> *I'd like to pass on a quote from Davis Love III which was given to me by Ken Brown before I went out for my first match in the 1977 Ryder Cup at Valderrama … 'let you attitude determine the game, don't let the game determine your attitude.'* [11]

> **Darren Clarke, Ryder Cup golfer**

Let's look at the tasks in the two tables on the next page. The principle behind these tasks is the relationship between *thinking*, *feeling* and *behaviour*. In simple terms, the way we *think*, affects the way we *feel*, which in turn affects our *behaviour*. It

Identify three challenges in your current life when you display a really positive and optimistic outlook in your mind. Make some notes describing the situation, how you feel and what the impact is on your performance

Challenge 1

Challenge 2

Challenge 3

Identify three challenges in your current life when you tend to display a negative and pessimistic outlook in your mind. Make some notes down describing the situation, how you feel and what the impact is on your performance

Challenge 1

Challenge 2

Challenge 3

therefore follows, that if we wish to change our behaviour, we need to influence our feelings, which is best done by modifying the way we think. Thinking pessimistically leads to feelings of negativity resulting in low confidence and poor performance. In contrast, an optimistic outlook leads to positive feelings, and hence higher confidence and superior performance. See how you get on completing the two tables and then reflect on how you can go about adopting a more optimistic outlook both specifically for the challenges you identify in the table below and more generally in the way you think about your life.

'KP' the optimist

The epitome of optimism among the Ashes winning England Cricket Team was Kevin Pietersen (nicknamed KP for obvious reasons). This is a player who is packed full of self belief which converts into a sense of optimism which can be passed on to team-mates. Ashley Giles reflected on the time he walked out to bat with KP in the final, and crucial, fifth match of the series. The position of the match, and series as a whole, was hanging in the balance but Giles described afterwards how Pietersen was 'absolutely brilliant ... he was so relaxed ... he was amazing.'

Optimism can certainly be infectious and as the old cliché goes – 'attitude is contagious, is yours worth catching?' KP seems to be a hard-wired optimist so it probably comes quite easy to him. Most people, though, have to work hard at maintaining a positive outlook, particularly when the going gets tough. Making the point of surrounding yourself by other optimists is a good start. If you find yourself constantly in the midst of pessimism and negativity you seriously run the risk of being dragged

In this team, whatever the situation, there is always someone who comes along and puts up his hand. Pietersen has a bit of genius to play like that. It was an extraordinary effort. The guy is so positive.[12]
Michael Vaughan, 2005 Ashes winning England Captain

down. So go and seek out the optimists. Pick their brains to find out how they think and how they deal with relentless pressure and the odds being stacked against them. Be inquisitive. You might have something to teach them about finance, procedures and other technical matters – but it just might be that you can learn from them when it comes to developing your Endurance Toughness through adopting a more optimistic outlook.

Highlights

In his book *Embracing Your Potential*, Canadian sport psychologist Professor Terry Orlick has an opening chapter entitled 'Capture the simple joys'. In it, he articulates the importance of actively embracing 'highlights' within your everyday life.

> *Positive realities live within the vision we choose to carry around within us. Life is full of extraordinary opportunities for embracing simple joys within ordinary experiences. Joyfulness lives within the magic of opening our minds and hearts to find joy in simplicity itself. Any occasion that can create feelings of intimacy, connection, worthiness, contribution, accomplishment, playfulness, balance, or tranquillity is a wonderful opportunity for embracing magical moments. We need only open our eyes, arms and hearts to experience more of these moments. Though some may last but a short time, they can bring pure joy and enchantment. I call such magical moments highlights.*[13]

Professor Terry Orlick, from *Embracing Your Potential*

Orlick's quote may seem misplaced in a book about mental toughness and appear a little too 'warm and fuzzy' but I maintain that his message is a very sound one. If you are trying to avoid getting run down and burned out by the relentless pressure and demands of your job (and perhaps even your life in general), then it makes perfect sense to me that you should actively focus on connecting with the highlights in your life. These will vary enormously from one person to the next but the process of identifying and embracing them is the same. Walking my dog in the fields near my home in the Cotswolds is definitely one of mine. Along with watching my younger daughter Morgan play soccer at the weekends. Simply chatting in the car with my teenage daughter Alexa about her current music tastes would count as well, as would going out for a coffee with my wife Donna. It's so easy to lose touch with these highlights when you're constantly on the run and feeling under pressure.

The other mistake people make is to be mentally elsewhere. In other words, you are physically present in a highlight situation but not able to really enjoy the moment because your mind is preoccupied with something else – usually a work-related issue or problem. Imagine reading a bedtime story to a child but all the time thinking about other things. Imagine being out on a country walk

You're only here for a short visit, so don't hurry, don't worry, and be sure to stop and smell the flowers along the way.[14]
Walter Hagen, former golf champion

with your dog but mentally being back in the office planning the meeting you will be in the following day. Imagine having a romantic dinner with your partner but being pretty boring company because your mind keeps drifting back to the report you haven't done for your boss yet. All these are perfect opportunities to embrace a highlight, but the moment is missed because you are mentally in the wrong place. Mentally tough individuals are good at being 'in the moment' – not just when they are performing but also when they are switched off and enjoying down time. They are able to really connect with the magic in a highlight moment and use the experience to refresh and recharge.

Be on the look out

I coach people to be on the look out for highlight opportunities. When you're feeling overwhelmed and exhausted due to the relentless pressure you are under it's crucial that you seek out opportunities to experience highlights. I advise people to actively set themselves 'highlight goals'. For example, experiencing two highlights a day for the next week. It is possible to do this even when you feel like you haven't got a minute to spare and everything seems like a real drag. Why not stop for a few seconds to enjoy some scenery? Pause a while to listen to the sounds of nature. Spend five minutes looking out of your hotel window at the city lights. Admire the view as your aeroplane lands. Take the time to listen to a piece of your favourite music whilst not doing anything else at the same time. Slow down and savour the tastes of your lunch without being on the phone or checking emails on your BlackBerry. Professor Terry Orlick claims that embracing highlights is an essential part of reducing stress, staying healthy and enjoying life more. Fundamentally it's about controlling your thinking. There's only one person in control of your thoughts – and that's you! Although you cannot control circumstances, you can control your reactions to them and how you go about maintaining a positive outlook. Focusing on, and embracing, highlights helps us to do this.

The table opposite gives you some further guidance on how you can think about highlights and challenge yourself to spend just several minutes each day embracing them.

If you genuinely cannot find the time each day to spend just a handful of minutes embracing the type of things that feature in this table then you will struggle to develop your Endurance Toughness. These are the very things that can help us navigate our way through challenging times and mentally tough

Highlight category	Examples
Enjoying nature	• Walking in the countryside • Listening to the birds • Admiring the natural beauty in a garden
Spending time with friends and family	• Reading your child a bedtime story • Having a relaxing drink with a friend • Half an hour of uninterrupted conversation with your partner
Listening to meaningful music	• A tune which reminds you of happy holiday memories • A tune which you find inspiring • A tune which you find deeply soothing
Being physically active	• A brisk walk at lunchtime • Taking an early morning jog • A bicycle ride
Observing something scenic	• The stars and city lights at night • A countryside view • A beautiful landscape painting
Savouring something sensual	• Your favourite coffee smell • A delicious meal • A five minute shoulder massage
Laughter and humour	• Enjoying a really funny joke • Reading something amusing in the newspaper • Watching an episode of your favourite comedy show on TV
Learning something	• Reading something informative in a magazine • Hearing something new and interesting from a friend • The opportunity to experience something for the first time

performers are acutely aware of the type of highlights that work for them. They then ensure that they have a plan in place to access these highlights as frequently as possible. They thereby maintain a positive outlook and cope much better with the relentless pressure of the day job. Consider the quote by Michael Vaughan in which he describes his friend Ashley Giles and how he is able to switch off from the day job and enjoy himself.

> *Ash is just a nice laid-back guy. I like his attitude, it's very similar to mine. He's very disciplined and profes-sional, but he knows when to relax. He can switch on and off. Not everyone can do that. He's tough on the field but he can enjoy himself too. We're very similar in that sense.*[15]

> **Michael Vaughan, speaking about his Ashes team-mate Ashley Giles**

In summary, highlights must feature in your mental toughness game plan somewhere in some form. It's up to you what they are and how you choose to embrace them. Just make sure you do.

Perspective

The third element of 'managing your outlook' is that of keep-ing things in perspective. When the pressure at work is piling up, deadlines are feeling overpowering and you cannot see any light at the end of the tunnel, it's critical that you somehow keep a balanced perspective. This is more than just the work–life balance challenge. It is about constantly keeping clear in your mind what the important things are in life. When you are going through a particularly difficult phase at work – like our IT Specialist Paul, who we discussed earlier in the chapter – it is natural to start to get bogged down by the constant demands and challenges of the job. It can start to feel like your whole 'self' is wrapped up in the job and that your feelings of belief and self-worth are a function of how you are performing at work. Although you know that other things are important too, you can't seem to really appreciate this to the extent that you know you should. My father had several adages that he drummed into me as a young boy. Things like 'it's better to be ten minutes early than two minutes late' or 'never put off to tomorrow what you can do today'. He spoke regularly about life's challenges being 'character building' and I recall as a teenager doing mundane jobs during vacation time, coming home and him explaining how these experiences would give me resilience in later life (he was right – of course!). To this day, we joke about events being 'character building' and, inevitably, as you might expect, I now find myself passing this message on to my own children in the hope that one day, they will come to realize the benefits of this type of resilient attitude. However, the one adage which has stuck with me the most over the years is the one he would use whenever, as a child, I started moaning about life's problems and feeling sorry for myself. He would consistently say – 'no matter how badly off you think you are, there's always someone else worse off than you.' Alan Mullaly is a former England cricketer who was always known for his relaxed and laid back approach to life. My father would whole-heartedly approve of his quote here.

> *I've got a philosophy that there are a lot of people in the world worse off than me. My worst day is if I get no wickets, so it's a great day compared to a lot of people I've seen on tour in South Africa and India. It's great to be alive, isn't it?* [16]

Alan Mullaly, former England cricketer

So the message is quite straightforward. When life is getting you down, when work is proving to be one hassle after the next, when the pressure seems relentless and never-ending, when your boss doesn't appreciate all the hard work you are putting in. Among many other things in your game plan, make sure you keep a perspective that reminds you of how fortunate you are in the grand scheme of things.

The legendary Brian Clough, a football manager remembered for his less-than-orthodox approach to dealing with players, regularly spoke of the importance of putting the game in the wider context of life. Apparently, in the early 1980s when managing Nottingham Forest, Clough took his players to the local coalfields to show them what he felt was 'real work' and how lucky they were to be professional footballers. On another occasion he postponed training one day to take the team to a high security prison to reinforce their good fortune.

Steve Waugh is the former captain of the Australian cricket team which held a pre-eminent position in world cricket in the ten years leading up to the Ashes series of 2005. Waugh himself is widely regarded as one of the mentally toughest cricketers of all time. In 1999, in consultation with Australia's army chief, Lieutenant General Peter Cosgrove, Waugh devised a plan for the Australian team to visit Anzac Grove in Gallipoli – the site of the World War I campaign in which over 8000 Australian soldiers were killed. Waugh and his team-mates stood up to their chests in a trench and reflected on the experience of being in a place that is considered sacred ground for Australians. Afterwards, Waugh commented that 'all teams should visit and immerse themselves in the spirit of the place' describing how, unsurprisingly, the experience had been deeply moving for them.

It certainly helps to retain a clear perspective on life when everything is not always smooth sailing, as well as ensuring that you enjoy the moment and not worry about the past or what might happen in the future. It's the present that counts and what you can control and therefore what you should be enjoying.[17]

Steve Waugh, former captain of the Australian cricket team and Australian of the year in 2004

Very soon after the Ashes series in 2005, the England Team embarked on what was going to be an exceedingly challenging tour of Pakistan. The players arrived in the country less than three weeks after the infamous Kashmir Earthquake in which around 100,000 people died and over three million lost their homes. Michael Vaughan spoke with great feeling prior to flying to Pakistan about how events such as this 'put things in perspective'. Before starting their cricket schedule, he and his team-mates then proceeded to engage in a number of hospital visits and contributions to the aid effort which they all found to be incredibly moving and humbling experiences. Their perspectives on dealing with the stresses and hassles of their day job were undoubtedly influenced – for the better. It was to hold them in good stead for what was about to follow – i.e. a long and arduous winter of travel, performance, challenge and pressure.

As an exercise in testing your ability to maintain appropriate perspective, consider what your personal triggers are for losing perspective. What are the types of things that lead you to relinquish your grasp on a balanced way of thinking about the stresses you are experiencing. Make a few notes in the table on the next page.

My triggers for losing perspective

-

-

-

-

-

Becoming aware of these triggers is the first step to doing something about them. Your triggers might be related to your working hours, the piling pressure you are experiencing working on a particular project over several months, the attitude of your boss, the challenge of getting your work–life balance right, etc. They will be different for all of us but you need to know exactly what yours are.

When you are aware of your triggers, then you can devise a plan for managing your outlook. This plan can have two parts. Firstly – what are the special things in your life that you should focus on and appreciate? – things that remind you of how fortunate you are. Secondly – what experiences could you give yourself to help you put things in perspective? – in other words, what's your equivalent of the footballers visiting a coal mine or the cricketers visiting a hospital? This next table prompts you again to make some notes on these two actions.

I must remember ...

-

-

-

Possible 'perspective' experiences I could gain ...

-

-

-

To conclude, the quote by Graham Thorpe summarizes this section of the book succinctly. Your attitude is your decision and no one else's. Think about how you manage your outlook and consider just how impactful some modifications might be. Imagine the performance impact of an outlook which was robustly optimistic, made the most of embracing 'highlights' and enabled a balanced perspective at all times. Now that would be the kind of attitude conducive to formulating a powerful mental toughness game plan!

No one can guarantee success on the field but you can guarantee your attitude off it.[18]

Graham Thorpe, former England cricketer

The Game Plan for Endurance Toughness

- Consider how you can get two or three extra 'small dose' activity sessions of several minutes duration per day.

- Reflect on your diet – is it helping or hindering you to manage your energy? Identify three changes you could make right now that would have an impact.

- Think about how you eat and energize when you're on the road. Choose just one thing from Fred's road warrior rules that you could start from the next trip you make.

- Try and do three 10/10 relaxation routines per week but if you only manage one or two, so be it – stick at it.

- Pick a couple of stressful situations in which you would benefit from using the three step quick-fire relaxation trick.

- Choose three current challenges you have where you need to show more optimism.

- Identify the kind of 'highlights' that you should focus on daily to help you manage your outlook as positively as possible.

- Make notes on (i) the special things in your life that help you to appreciate how fortunate you are, as well as (ii) 'perspective' experiences that you could gain.

Risk Management Toughness

6

Lifelong learners take risks. Much more than others, these men and women push themselves out of their comfort zones and try new ideas. While most of us become set in our ways, they keep experimenting.[1]

Professor John Kotter, Harvard Business School and author of *Leading Change*

John Kotter is considered by many to be the world's foremost expert on business leadership. His quote about lifelong learners, taken from his acclaimed book *Leading Change* (p.182) could equally be applied to mentally tough performers. Elite performance, no matter what the context, is about pushing boundaries and finding small margins here and there. This requires an element of risk taking. You don't generally win gold medals by playing it safe or taking the conservative option. You have to push to the limits and back yourself to deliver. This does not, however, mean that mentally tough performers are reckless or take risks without planning. They make rational decisions based on a strong sense of self-belief around the wisdom of their decision and their ability to execute against it. They know their own strengths and limitations and their

The ability to make the right decision – and then dare to do the right thing in all situations – is decisive at the top of the modern game.[2]
Sven-Goran Eriksson, former Coach of the England football team

risk management is based on this well-developed self-awareness.

This type of mental toughness tends to be displayed in people who are constantly seeking to test themselves. Graham Gooch, arguably the most successful batsman English cricket has ever produced, is well known for a story in which he was playing for his county side, Essex, against the touring West Indies team in their pomp. Apparently, on the morning of the match, news reached the Essex locker room that Malcolm Marshall, the legendary fast bowler who sadly died in 1999, was not to be playing in the game. On hearing this news, the general feeling in the room was one of relief due to Marshall's potency as an opening bowler. Gooch, on the other hand, is remembered for his own reaction which was one of disappointment – he wanted to play against the best in the world and was being deprived of this opportunity with the absence of Marshall. This is Risk Management Toughness at its best. Wanting to put your reputation on the line and compete against the best is borne out of a love of challenge … and so to Tip 8.

TIP 8: SEEK OUT THE CHALLENGE

When you are excited by the challenge of competition or having to prove yourself under pressure you will approach risk management in a more confident and positive manner. You are more focused on the enjoyment of success rather than the fear of failure. This is a sometimes quite subtle but extremely powerful distinction. Being motivated by fear of failure is not generally a recipe for mental toughness. Elite performers are motivated by the thrill of performing in difficult circumstances and demonstrating their abilities when the odds are against them. In short, they just love a challenge. This is as true in business as it is in sport but as an interesting example look at the quote by Billy Bowden who was one of the officials involved in the 2005 Ashes series. His quote illustrates how he wanted to be tested – it's exactly the mindset that Graham Gooch possessed.

> *When I came home for the Fifth Test for a break, I was hoping Australia would need to win the last Test. I wanted to be among it, in the middle, with team one and two in the world – and I wanted to be tested.*[3]

> **Billy Bowden, international cricket umpire speaking about the 2005 Ashes series**

So the recommendation here goes back to the old cliché about threat and opportunity. Winners usually see challenges in terms of an opportunity to test themselves and prove something. Losers, on the other hand, default to seeing all the threats inherent in the challenge and develop anxiety around the possibility of things going wrong. Consequently they will not choose risky options even when the situation requires them to do so because they are fearful of failure.

Gary's story

One of my very early (and most interesting) assignments as a sport psychologist was when I worked with an athlete called Gary Shopland. Gary was an ultra-distance runner – a collective term essentially given to athletes who run endurance events longer than the conventional marathon (i.e. 26.2 miles). A couple of years before I was introduced to him, Gary had attempted to navigate the length of the Andes mountain range on foot. However, by his own admission, his expedition was poorly prepared and he failed – having to be airlifted off a mountain by helicopter to safety. His downfall had been heat exhaustion and he was bitterly disappointed to have been beaten by the elements. So, not long after his recovery, he began contemplating his next challenge. Having been beaten by the heat in the Andes, he was determined to prove to himself that he could cope with extreme temperatures and so decided that he would complete a 500 mile run through the deserts of California and Nevada at the hottest time of the year. He set himself the challenge of completing a marathon a day for 20 days and to complete the enormity of the expedition, along the way he was to incorporate the infamous Death Valley – a 130 mile stretch of land surrounded by steep mountain ranges. Air temperatures in Death Valley during the month of July (Gary's chosen time for the expedition) are frequently in excess of 50 degrees Celsius and to remind you of the hostile nature of the environment there are points of interest named Desolation Canyon, Dante's View, Badwater, Devil's Canyon and Funeral Mountain. It is a spectacular place and was described by David Attenborough on the BBC's *Planet Earth* series as the 'hottest place on earth'.

Gary's perspective was that, having failed to conquer the heat in his previous expedition, he was compelled to raise the bar and now challenge himself in a way that would demonstrate his ability to deal with the extreme environmental conditions which had been his downfall. It was to be a risk. Death Valley can be an incredibly dangerous place. On the Wikitravel website it states *'Follow Desert Survival guidelines. The name of the park says it all. People have died within the borders.'* Gary would not be stopping in hotels for a good night's sleep and pampering. There would be no such establishments in the middle of the desert. He was to stop on the roadside exactly where his day's running finished and sleep in the recreational vehicle which would be his only source of refuge from the hostile environment outside.

Gary knew that he couldn't complete the challenge without some form of back-up support so he recruited three specialists to work with him in the 12 weeks preceding the run, and then accompany him during the expedition itself. He chose an exercise scientist who would be responsible for monitoring all the physiological aspects of his training and performance. This would include managing his fluid intake, dietary needs and the content of his physical preparation. Second, was a former army paramedic who was present for medical emergencies as well as for looking after route planning and navigation. I was the third member of the support team – his sport psychologist. My responsibilities focused on helping Gary devise, develop and stick to his game plan. Yes, he most definitely had a game plan and it was a very thorough one too. It involved daily goal setting, positive self-talk, visualization, concentration strategies and use of a personalized version of the 10/10 relaxation routine at the end of each day's running

Accompanying Gary on the event itself was a fascinating adventure and not without incident. The route was to start and finish at Caesar's Palace in Las Vegas. The first few days were fairly straightforward but then the air-conditioning system in our vehicle broke down which meant Gary had nowhere to cool down between running stints. It was difficult sleeping at night. We came face to face with rattlesnakes, scorpions and various other forms of wildlife to which we were not accustomed. Temperatures were as blisteringly hot as we could have imagined. I recall on one particular day in the middle of Death Valley, Gary consumed around 15 litres of fluid whilst passing only 0.25 litre of urine. At the end of each day's running his body was a wreck. He would literally hobble from the roadside, onto the weighing scales (a twice daily ritual implemented by the exercise scientist to check for significant weight loss which would have signalled the onset of extreme dehydration and heat exhaustion), and then into the vehicle. At the start of each day's running he looked as if he was in absolute agony (probably because he was!) as he shuffled along the road gradually loosening stiffness from his legs as he embarked on another 26 miles under the scorching midday sun.

To cut to the end of a very long story, Gary did it. He successfully completed 500 miles and even managed to reach Las Vegas in 19 days – one day ahead of schedule. There were no crowds to cheer him in and no real interest from anyone on the busy streets other than the BBC film crew (who were making a documentary about the event) and ourselves. This was of no concern to Gary though. He had achieved his goal. He had set himself the challenge with all the associated risks inherent in such an undertaking. He had endured all the pain, as well as the boredom. Through a process of rigorous preparation, unshakeable self-belief and remarkable mental toughness he had done it. He had felt compelled to 'seek out the challenge' following the disappointment of his previous adventure. And now his achievement desire had been satiated – temporarily at least!

When Gary invited me to work with him I was in my first year as a university lecturer. A number of my colleagues strongly advised me *not* to get involved. They said it was too much of a professional risk – particularly so early in my career (I was 27 at the time). They feared that Gary could seriously harm himself and even die if things went really badly. They suggested that this would tarnish my future career prospects and at that stage in my professional life I would be better off doing something rather more conventional. I chose not to take their advice – well intentioned as it was. I accepted the risks involved but wanted to test myself in my chosen field. Could I really do this 'sport psychologist' thing – not just in the laboratory or the class-room but also out in the 'real world'? Both the challenge and the opportunity to learn excited and intrigued me, and I have never regretted the decision I made. In fact, it made many of the professional challenges I have faced in the intervening 20 years seem much easier. I have never, for instance, had to break off from a coaching session with anyone sitting on a rock in the middle of a desert because we spotted a rattlesnake curled up less than a metre from our feet!

Be hungry for feedback

Another angle on seeking challenge as a way in which you can develop your mental toughness is to actively seek out feed-back. Elite performers, whether they are in sport or business, are generally very keen on receiving feedback because they realize how important it is to performance improvement. If you are wishing to raise your performance bar then you need to be very aware of your strengths and development needs. Feedback is a crucial way of acquiring this information but, of course, asking for feedback can be a risky business – you might not like what you hear! Nevertheless, mental toughness is about taking risks – as long as they're the right risks. So, I would actively encourage you to get feedback on a regular basis. This is what elite athletes get if you think about it. They work with their coaches most days and get feedback constantly – on their practice, on their training runs, on their attitude, on the fitness, on their diet, on their preparation and of course on their match performance. It's not like this in business though. You are often left on your own for much of the time and although this can be appealing, in terms of independence and autonomy, it can lead to individuals going weeks and months without receiving any really useful feedback. If this is your situation, then I am urging you to be proactive in requesting feedback. You may not always like what you hear, but you should be able to learn something really useful from it. Adopting such an approach towards your performance development is definitely a demonstration of mental toughness.

Managing your reactions to feedback

Clearly, not all the feedback that you will receive will be unquestionably positive. You are likely to receive some feedback on occasions that you either don't like or don't agree with. Managing your reactions to this is also a part of the mental toughness process. The acronym SADRAA is my personal favourite for explaining the type of stages people go through when they receive feedback that they might not be particularly happy with. The table opposite explains how these letters describe six distinct phases that people often experience when receiving difficult feedback.

When writing SADRAA on a flipchart during workshops, I often colour code the six letters as I have indicated in the left hand column. Shock, anger and denial are all part of an emotional response which is often quite strong and negative – hence the 'red zone'. Rationalization and acceptance are thinking related and are about eventually coming to terms with the feedback in a constructive and considered manner – I call this the 'blue zone' due to it being rather more mellow and calm than the previous phases. Finally, the 'green zone' is about action – i.e. changing behaviour. Having understood the feedback and appreciated

The 'red' zone **Emotions**	**S**	HOCK	'Wow – I did not expect that! I'm really surprised by those comments.'
	A	NGER	'How dare they say that. Wait till I get the chance to get my own back!'
	D	ENIAL	'I'm not like that at all. I don't behave like that. I can't understand why they would pick that out.'
The 'blue' zone **Thinking**	**R**	ATIONALIZATION	'Yes but the reason they think that is because they don't know what kind of pressure I am under. Anyway, that's the way I am and why should I change? Look at my performance – I'm certainly delivering the numbers aren't I?'
The 'green' zone **Behaviour**	**A**	CCEPTANCE	'OK – I accept that I need to change.'
	A	CTION	'Right, what is my action plan? I am seriously committed to developing my performance by using this feedback in the most practical, and useful, way I can. I shall start tomorrow.'

its value (even if you may not have liked it at first) you are now ready to implement plans to change your approach and hence raise your performance level. Mentally tough performers get through these six phases as quickly as they can. They don't dwell too long in the early phases of shock, anger, denial and rationalization. They move swiftly towards accepting the feedback and deciding how it can help them achieve their goals.

Consider now how you could increase your Risk Management Toughness by becoming more feedback hungry. Use the table to help you record some notes for a plan to acquire feedback. Don't simply choose your friends at work to give you feedback – pick people who you respect and who will give you honest and practical views.

WHO	WHEN and HOW	ON WHAT
Three people, whose views I respect, who I could ask for some feedback	When is the best time to ask for their help and what format should they use – written or verbal?	Specifically, what shall I ask each for feedback on? It may well be different for each individual

A final tip on the feedback process is to ensure that you get feedback on your strengths as well as your development needs. It's really important that you learn to maximize your strengths as well as managing your weaknesses so make sure that you devote quality time to assessing the extent to which your are doing this.

Ashes 2005

England have to make a major decision for the Oval Test. Do they go for a draw or a win? They will be making a mistake if they settle for the former. Everything should be geared to winning this one. That way they can maintain the positive momentum they have established in the first four Ashes Tests.[4]

Raymond Illingworth, former Ashes winning England cricket captain

As already explained earlier in the book, England were holding a 2–1 lead going into the final match of the 2005 Ashes series. A draw would therefore be good enough for them to regain the trophy and end the 18 year Australian reign. However, opting to play for the draw has often led to teams coming unstuck and losing the game through overly tentative and conservative play. Raymond Illingworth alludes to this point in his quote by stating the importance of maintaining the winning momentum. However, by playing to win, by definition, you are also accepting a greater risk of losing so this is where Risk Management Toughness becomes crucial. However, the mindset of many elite athletes is that it is more about 'making a decision' rather than 'taking a risk'. They genuinely don't see things in terms of risk but simply in terms of what they have to do – i.e. go for the challenge.

The hardest thing for England will be to isolate the game from its context. At no stage must they allow themselves to think, 'the Ashes are at stake'. The players must stick to the positive approach that has got them to this point and believe in it because it is working.[5]

David Gower, former England Cricket captain and SKY Sports presenter

The message in David Gower's quote is straightforward. He advises against thinking about the consequences of losing the game. Instead his view is that the players should simply focus on the positive approach that has been working for them throughout the summer. As it turned out, England chose to play positively and go for the win although the final result was to be a famous draw – enabling England to regain the Ashes.

And finally ...

Despite the general message within this tip, the attitude I am describing is not about wild abandonment and throwing caution to the wind at every available opportunity. Clearly there are times in life (and certainly at work) when we have to take a safe option. There are many risks that it is absolutely better not to take and it would be foolish to do otherwise. Nevertheless, this tip is about seeking out the challenge as a way of, in the words of John Kotter, getting 'out of the comfort zone' and this is very much part of Risk Management Toughness.

Many sports coaches talk passionately about wanting athletes on their team who are prepared to stand up and be counted. In other words, performers who actively want the chance to win the game. This is a risk of course. They are putting themselves, and their reputations, on the line. I find the same phenomenon in my corporate work. Time and time again I hear CEOs, Vice Presidents and Directors talk about wanting 'players' in the business – individuals who are not only 'prepared' to test themselves but actively 'want' to.

So come on. Love the challenge. Seek it out. View it as an opportunity, not a threat and you'll be far better placed to manage your risk taking. You'll feel more confident to 'go for it' and you'll have fun in the process! Think how you can test yourself in the coming weeks and months. How can you push yourself out of your comfort zone and stretch your abilities? Consider situations where you can 'flip' your thinking, take personal responsibility and view the challenge as an exciting opportunity rather than an inconvenient threat. This will develop your Risk Management Toughness. In the words of the well-known Accenture company's advertising boards – 'Go on. Be a Tiger'.

TIP 9: REFRAME YOUR APPRAISAL

In addition to their open-top bus tour of the city of London, the England Cricket Team were also awarded MBEs (and an OBE for Michael Vaughan the captain) for their heroic efforts in regaining the Ashes in 2005. Look at the quote from Kevin Pietersen (remember 'KP the optimist' from earlier in the book) about the experience of receiving his award at Buckingham Palace. He suddenly found himself in a strangely unfamiliar world of not being confident and his mind started creating anxiety which then translated into physical symptoms. Nice to know he sweats like the rest of us when he's unsure of himself – which is a very rare occurrence!

> *In all my life, my hands have never been perspiring as much as they did when I went up to get that award. In the whole series, even on the last day at the Oval, I was not as nervous as that.*[6]

> **Kevin Pietersen, comparing receiving his MBE from the Queen with playing in the 2005 Ashes series**

So what's going on here? How can such a confident young man appear so nervous? With a cricket bat in his hand, he is the archetypal warrior athlete but when faced with making small talk with Her Majesty he is reduced to a bag of nerves!

Let's answer that question by reviewing the way in which appraisal influences the stress process. For more than 20 years now, it has been widely accepted amongst psychologists that appraisal plays a key role in the stress and coping process. In large part, this acceptance is the result of the work of Professor Richard Lazarus from the University of California, Berkeley. He published a book with Dr Susan Folkman in 1984 called *Stress, Appraisal and Coping*, which went on to become one of the most widely read and cited academic books in the psychology research world. The basic premise of the book, which emanated from the authors' own research, was that people suffer stress and anxiety when they feel they lack the resources to cope. This may sound obvious at first but the implications are profound. Throughout his illustrious career Professor Lazarus repeatedly demonstrated that it is not the environment alone that causes stress but rather the way in which the individual interacts with his or her environment – and most notably, the role that appraisal plays in this interaction process. By definition, therefore, if someone can change their appraisal of a stressful situation and enhance their belief that they can cope, then any inherent stress will be dissipated.

To illustrate this point, let me now provide you with a personal anecdote relating to the first time I travelled in an aeroplane.

My aeroplane story

When I was 14 my family took a foreign holiday for the first time. We were off to Switzerland and had to fly from London's Heathrow airport to Basel. I was extremely excited about the prospect of air travel and the trip was not to disappoint me. As it happened, the flight was delayed for a few hours and consequently it necessitated a night-time landing. Approximately half an hour before landing the heavens opened and we found ourselves in the middle of a massive thunderstorm. It was like nothing I have experienced since in over 30 years of flying. Lightning bolts were striking what seemed like right outside the window. The wings looked as if they were going to snap off at any moment. The turbulence was akin to a massive rollercoaster and the flight attendants were firmly strapped in their seats looking a shade uncomfortable (never a good sign). As we began the final descent to landing I felt the wheels drop from the undercarriage and moments later I could see the runway a matter of metres below us through the window to my right. At the very last possible moment the plane suddenly started to ascend again and bank to the left. The captain was heard over the public address system … 'I'm very sorry ladies and gentlemen but had we landed then we would have overshot the runway. I'll just circle and try again.' I was, at the time, blissfully unaware of the mountains at the end of the runway which no doubt would have been our buffer in the event of overshooting and consequently I continued to admire the wonderful sights I was witnessing outside – a river, lights, buildings, lightning thunderbolts. It was great! 'Look, Dad', I remember saying. 'Look at that down there'. I remember his response being less than enthusiastic as he tightly gripped his arm rest. Meanwhile we attempted to land another two times and eventually made it to rapturous applause from the relieved passengers who had been clutching their vomit bags for the past 45 minutes. As far as I was concerned the whole thing had been an exciting adventure from start to finish – even the long delay at Heathrow! I thought all flights were like this – great stuff – just like a rollercoaster only better and longer. Much longer. I can honestly say that I did not experience any stress, anxiety or concern at all. I was genuinely in a state of well-being and enthusiasm. Were I to experience exactly the same event today – having travelled by air many times since, my emotions and physical state would be completely different. Why? Simply because, on the basis of knowledge and experience, my thinking would be different. I would be aware of the possible dangers and probably would get sucked into thinking the worst, getting anxious and behaving in a very different way from when I was a teenager. In short, as Professor Lazarus demonstrated, my appraisal of the situation was instrumental in determining how I would react. It's not the situation itself that causes stress. It's how we think about it.

So, let's return to Kevin Pietersen. How was he appraising the notion of spending time in Buckingham Palace, and having to say and do all the right things in the presence of the Queen? How equipped did he feel? What resources did he have to draw on? His appraisal process would probably have highlighted the fact that he had never done anything like this before, did not have the knowledge, experience or resources to think on his feet, and the chances were that he would muck it up.

Kirsten Barnes is a Canadian former double Olympic Gold Medallist and World Champion rower. After Kirsten retired from her sport following the Barcelona Olympics in 1992, she trained to become a sport psychologist and studied for a PhD. The conclusion of any PhD study programme involves a very rigorous and searching interview with two or three examiners – referred to as a 'viva'. All students find this experience fairly harrowing but I can recall discussing the matter with Kirsten who explained how much more nervous she was entering this 'viva' situation than she had ever been sitting on the start line of an Olympic or World Championship final. So again, this illustrates the point. Kirsten was worried about the situation because she was unsure of the demands that would be placed upon her and her ability to cope. In the Olympic final, she knew what the demands were going to be and was confident in her inner coping resources.

To summarize, let's quote Shakespeare in *Hamlet*: 'There is nothing either good or bad, but thinking makes it so.' Therefore, change the way we think about a stressful situation and we can change the emotional reaction we have to it and hence we will influence our self-confidence. In turn, we will be managing our risk-taking from a different perspective. We will have a far stronger base from which to take a risky option or stretch ourselves. But in order to do this effectively we must challenge, and then reframe, our appraisal.

How do we do it?

In simple terms we can challenge our appraisal processes from three different perspectives. To understand these, let's consider what it is that we appraise when faced with a potentially stressful situation. As an example, think about when you are contemplating applying for a promotion within your company. You really would love this new job but you are also aware that it's a big step up and you don't believe that your boss will support your application. Are you really good enough to get the job? It will be a 'risk' submitting an application because whilst the prospect of success is very appealing, what about if you don't even get shortlisted? Will your confidence be dented? Will your colleagues think that you are arrogant to assume that you even had a chance in the first place? What if you do get an interview but perform so badly that you scupper your chances of getting promoted sometime in the future? Do you take the risk? What goes on in your mind?

Step 1: DEMANDS

The first thing we appraise when contemplating this course of action are the demands of the situation. How difficult will the process be? Will the interview be too much of a challenge? How much time will filling out the application take? Will my boss react negatively to my intentions?

Step 2: ABILITY

Next we appraise our ability to meet these demands. Do I have the skills to do the job? Will I perform well at the interview? How good is my CV? In short – do I feel able to carry it off?

Step 3: CONSEQUENCES

Finally, we also appraise the consequences of the perform-ance outcome. What will happen if I am successful? What will happen if I fail? How much will success mean to me and how disastrous will it be if I fail?

In terms of taking a risk, you can figure out that we are most likely to do so under conditions where we feel the demands are low, our ability is high and the consequences are not overly sig-nificant. Regrettably, though, in many situations our appraisal processes do not play out in that way. Rather, we perceive the demands to be high and the consequences significant whilst not feeling particularly confident in our ability. The net result of this is stress, anxiety and a reluctance to take a risk. And in our example of going for the promotion – at the last minute we change our minds and decide not to go for it after all.

So, modifying the way in which we appraise these three areas can influence our attitude towards seeking out challenge, test-ing ourselves and taking a risk. Ideally, we're aiming for an appraisal process that results in us perceiving demands as being not too high, our ability as being very high and the consequences as being manageable (important perhaps but not the end of the world). The table below illustrates how we can start to question our appraisal by challenging the beliefs that we are holding about a situation.

Reframing self-dcfeating statements

Challenging	Appraisal
Demands (need to create a reduced perception)	Is this really as difficult as I am making it out to be? Let's break this down and analyse exactly what is being asked of me Why am I thinking this is so difficult?
Ability (need to create an increased perception)	What have I achieved in the past that was similar to this challenge? Who else has performed well in this situation that I can learn from? Come on, remember how important positive thinking is!
Consequences (need to create a more balanced perspective)	What's the worst thing that could happen here? There are more important things in my life than this right now Come on, nothing ventured nothing gained!

Now think about how you could apply this reappraisal process to situations that you are, or will be, facing which will require you to be bold enough to take a risk and put yourself on the line – such as challenging your boss, applying for a job or addressing a conflict that you have been having with a colleague. In each of these situations, if you can reduce the perceived demand, increase your perceived ability and have a more balanced perspective on the consequences then you are far more likely to display Risk Management Toughness.

Hannah's story

Hannah worked for a consulting company and her story is an example of how changing thinking can quickly impact on risk management. I coached Hannah for a few months recently and during one coaching session we were focusing specifically on self-belief. As we began discussing the topic she explained that she was really hoping to get a promotion later in the year which would mean she would be a partner in the company. She explained that there would probably be ten individuals in the running and that perhaps only three would be successful. She knew that it was not her strength to network and push herself forward in the way that she would have to in order to make an impression on the partners that would be making the appointments. I asked her to be more specific and she proceeded to explain that a certain large meeting which happened every other month was a perfect opportunity to raise her profile but there were usually around 100 people involved in these meetings and her natural inclination was to sit at the back and not have the confidence to contribute anything. She acknowledged that this had to change but did not know what to do. Together, we devised a quick plan based around three things. First, she needed to devote some quality time to preparing a question she could contribute to the deliberations within the meeting – this would involve doing some background reading, considering her options and then deciding on a question that she could ask at a certain point in the proceedings. Second, she needed to mentally rehearse herself asking the question (recall the section on visualization in the Critical Moment Toughness chapter) in advance of the meeting – just like an athlete preparing for a race. Third, she needed to reframe how she thought about delivering the question when it came to showtime. I asked her to tell me what typical thoughts she would have in a situation like this immediately preceding the event. The table on the next page displays the

Reframing self-defeating statements

Hannah's three negative thoughts	Steve's suggested replacements
'I'm worried about getting my words right. I hope I don't stutter and mix it all up. I'll sound completely incompetent.'	'If I speak slowly and deliberately, I'll be fine. Just as I have rehearsed.'
'I wonder if my question is really any good. I might be completely missing the point.'	'I've planned this question thoroughly. It's definitely the right question to ask.'
'I wonder what people will think of me. They'll probably wonder what I'm on about.'	'This question will have real impact. I think they'll be pretty impressed. I'm looking forward to the opportunity of showing people what I'm made of.'

type of self statements she would normally have as well as the ones that I suggested she replace them with. You can see for yourself how the reframing has taken place.

After we had completed this reframing process, Hannah felt completely different about asking this question in the forth-coming meeting. Previously she had felt reluctant to speak up due to a lack of confidence and hence was not prepared to take the risk. With a game plan in place involving good preparation, she no longer perceived the action as a risk. She intended to sit at the front of the room and seize her opportunity when it arose.

Crooked thinking

Of course, the process of reframing appraisal is not always as straightforward as it was with Hannah. Often it is made much more difficult by the tendency that many of us have to engage in more general self-defeating thoughts that seriously hamper our ability to think straight. Much of the current thinking in this area can be traced back to the original work of the world famous psychologist, Dr Albert Ellis, who is the author over 75 books and the creator of Rational Emotive Behaviour Therapy. Ellis, and many others since, has published a wealth of literature addressing the inhibiting role of, what has now been termed by some, 'crooked thinking'. We are all probably guilty of engaging in crooked thinking at certain times of our lives but Ellis and his followers strongly maintain that it militates against appropriate appraisal of challenging situations. In other words it will act as a barrier to clear thinking and good decision making. Again, there is an obvious need for reframing.

Crooked thinking can take various forms and the table opposite provides a brief summary of six different types, which I am sure you will recognize as either having used yourselves or witnessed in others. These types of thinking are absolutely not conducive to the kind of appraisal I have been discussing during this section of the book. In fact they will usually result in the opposite of what we are trying to achieve by (i) increasing perception of demand, (ii) decreasing perception of ability and (iii) leading to an inappropriate perception of consequence.

Having reviewed the six different types of crooked thinking, it's now important to consider when you are inclined towards falling into the trap of this type of negativity. Identify a situation in the past where you have perhaps employed each of the six types. The table on p.140 will help you do this.

Crooked thinking type (Adapted from the work of Albert Ellis)	Examples of related self-defeating statements
1.'Not fair' thinking	'Things really shouldn't be like this. It's not fair. I don't deserve this treatment.'
2. 'Driver' thinking	'I absolutely must perform well tomorrow to avoid disastrous results. If I don't deliver it will be a total catastrophe.'
3. 'Stopper' thinking	'I'm useless. I can't do it. I'm going to screw things up.'
4. 'Illogical' thinking	'If this happens then that will surely follow. If I make a mistake then they will hold it against me for ages.'
5. 'Blaming' thinking	'It's his fault. It's her fault. It's their fault. It's everyone's fault. It's not my fault.'
6. 'Overgeneralizing' thinking	'I NEVER get any breaks. This ALWAYS happens to me. EVERYTHING is going wrong in my life right now.'

It's so important for you to be aware of when you slip into crooked thinking and immediately you sense it happening to do something to stop and reframe the thought into a positive alternative.

This is essential if you are wishing to think your way clearly through a stressful situation requiring an element of risk. Furthermore, Dr Albert Ellis would advocate that you have to be hard on yourself in your self-talk. You are attempting to control your own thoughts and although you're the only person who can do this, it's not always a straightforward process. Look at the Nick Faldo quote illustrating just how inwardly aggressive he gets with himself when he's perhaps being lured towards crooked thinking or simply concentrating on the wrong things.

Crooked thinking type	Illustration	Personal example
'Not fair'	'It's just not fair that I have to make this presentation. I shouldn't be put under this much pressure to perform right now.'	
'Driver'	'I absolutely *have* to deliver tomorrow or else my reputation will take a massive dive and I'll never be able to retrieve it.'	
'Stopper'	'I'm useless in top team meetings and never have the confidence to challenge Mike – I just can't seem to bring myself to risk it.'	
'Illogical'	'If I make a mistake at the sales pitch next week then Jane will never invite me to accompany her on a client visit again.'	
'Blaming'	'Melissa always makes me feel nervous in meetings and I lose my train of thought. It's all her fault that I sounded like a gibbering idiot.'	
'Overgeneralizing'	'There's no point in me trying for that promotion that's coming up next month – I never get any breaks around here. They always choose someone from marketing for that type of position.'	

My game depends on focus and concentration. While I am playing I am talking to myself inside my head the whole time issuing verbal commands to myself. Sometimes the conversation comes out and I'll literally be talking to myself. I'll be saying 'Right' – I say 'right' a lot – 'Right, come on, get the f*** on with it, concentrate you dick. Go on, get back in there, my son. Rotate, turn, hit.' [7]

Nick Faldo, six times Major winner and Britain's greatest ever golfer

Of course, it's easier to slip into crooked thinking when you are tired or feeling under the weather so here's another reason for you to implement the advice presented in the Endurance Toughness chapter on staying fit and healthy by being active and eating well.

So, to summarize, the way you appraise a situation will determine your reaction to it. I established earlier that people who display Risk Management Toughness love to test themselves. They actively seek challenge and in so doing, they appraise the situation using straight rather than crooked thinking. This allows them to think clearly and manage any risks with confidence and a determination to succeed. Reframing any self-defeating thoughts you may have about a risky or pressurized situation is an essential part of your mental toughness game plan. If you can do this effectively, you will find that you will think much more clearly and make the right decisions at the right times.

Although the 2003 team probably peaked nine months before the World Cup, they did their job because they had enough players of authority on the field to make the right decisions at the right time to get the right results.[8]

Keith Wood, former Captain of the Ireland Rugby Team speaking about the 2003 World Cup winning England rugby side

---

The Game Plan for Risk Management Toughness

- Consider some situations where you could adopt a more 'seek out the challenge' kind of attitude – set yourself a goal of doing this at least three times in the next three months.

- Be hungry for feedback – create opportunities which allow you to receive feedback from your peers and boss as well as from direct reports if you have them.

- Pick three challenges which require you to reframe your appraisal of them – devise a specific plan for creating a positive mindset.

- Check yourself for crooked thinking and ensure that you know what type of thoughts need to be in place when you feel yourself slipping into a self-defeating thought pattern.

The Winning Environment

Ability gets you part of the way, hard work and preparation are fundamental, but it is the creation of a winning environment that really makes the difference.[1]

**Marcus Trescothick, vice-captain of the 2005
Ashes winning England Cricket Team**

The quote by Marcus Trescothick captures the essence of this chapter succinctly. If business leaders want people in their organization to demonstrate a winning approach to mental toughness, it is essential that they pay close attention to the kind of environment they are creating. A winning environment does not just happen on its own. Leaders need to take conscious steps to create an atmosphere where people can actively develop their performance skills and establish thinking habits which will foster self-belief, clear decision-making and resilience.

We've known for years now that people need to feel valued and appreciated in the workplace. Most companies employ some sort of engagement survey from time to time to check how connected the employees are feeling and how much organizational commitment they are inclined to demonstrate. However, these macro assessments of staff loyalty are not measuring whether, at a micro level, people are operating within a winning environment. I like to ask people what kind of 'vapour' hangs over their team in the workplace. Is it a vapour that facilitates a winning approach to mental toughness or one that is debilitating? How conducive is the immediate environment to the development of robust levels of self-belief whereby people maintain confidence and a positive outlook even when times are tough? In what ways does the environment contribute to good, clear decision-making and straight (rather than crooked) thinking? And how resilient do people feel? Are they able to withstand the stresses and strains of corporate life whilst delivering improved levels of efficiency and performance year on year? The environment is critical in influencing all of these processes and therefore team leaders must be constantly aware of the impact (both positive and negative) that they can have on shaping it.

You may, or may not, be fortunate enough to work for a visionary leader who is skillful in creating the kind of environment that fosters the development of optimal performance and winning ways. Either way, I'd like to encourage you to take personal responsibility for creating your own winning environment and it is this suggestion that is my 10th tip.

TIP 10: CREATE YOUR OWN WINNING ENVIRONMENT

If you have followed the advice from the previous nine tips you will be well on the way to creating your own winning environment but I now want to focus on three straightforward actions capable of providing you with quick wins – whether it be in the boardroom, warehouse or back office. I'm going to call these three quick wins: (1) the role thing, (2) playing to strengths, and (3) enjoying the ride. Let's look at them each in turn.

Quick Win 1: The Role Thing

In a famous episode of my favourite TV sitcom *Fawlty Towers*, Basil engages in one of his spectacular rants during which he suggests that Sybil, his wife, should enter *Mastermind* as a contestant and choose the 'bleedin' obvious' as her specialist topic. This characteristic irony was a result of Sybil stating something which Basil felt was so patently obvious that it didn't need articulating. I imagine that Basil may have the same reaction on reading this part of the book. Much of what I shall present is indeed fairly obvious but my consultancy experience has repeatedly led me to believe that, in the area of team roles, much is often taken for granted and leaders frequently assume that they do not have to spend time on 'the role thing' because everyone knows what their role is and are busy getting on with things. I have found this not to be the case in both sport and business performance contexts and hence my advice to business leaders is to be very careful about making assumptions relating to role functioning. The figure below presents a framework for explaining what needs to happen in order that role functioning can positively contribute to the creation of a winning environment. *Role clarity* sits at the base of the triangle. This refers to the need for you to be absolutely clear about what your role is exactly.

Role functioning

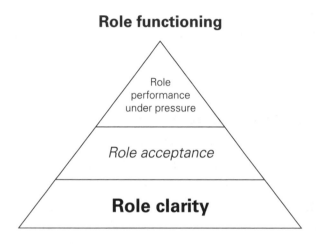

You need to have a sense of clarity relating to the day-to-day execution of your role as well as how your role may change during difficult times. I have frequently encountered situations where people are a little unsure of what they are expected to do but are unwilling to ask for fear of appearing incompetent. Consequently they bumble along doing the best they can until such time as their lack of clarity causes a significant error or misjudgement resulting in poor performance. It's crucial that you take the time to discuss role clarity with your boss and if he or she is not forthcoming then you should manage upwards by taking the initiative.

Next, consideration should be given to *role acceptance*. It may well be that you are very clear about your role and what is expected of you but you are not particularly comfortable with the role. You may not feel equipped to execute the role effectively or feel that your talents could be better exploited doing something else. Feelings of this nature are not conducive to the development of a winning environment and must be addressed.

When strong *role clarity* and *role acceptance* are firmly in place, the platform is present for execution and hence the top tier of the triangle – *role performance under pressure.* It is entirely logical (or 'bleedin' obvious' as Basil Fawlty would say!) that if individuals are totally clear about what their role is and feel very comfortable and happy in that role then they are more likely to perform well under pressure. Additionally, if each individual in a team is clear about, and happy with, the roles of their colleagues then they are more likely to be in a position to offer something constructive and supportive during challenging times. This process is a great way to develop team cohesion in addition to enhancing individual levels of mental toughness which is, of course, another important dimension of a winning environment.

To facilitate 'the role thing' within a team environment, I frequently conduct an interactive exercise designed to create meaningful conversations among team members. I call it 'role kites' and it can be implemented quite quickly in either formal or informal settings.

Role kite

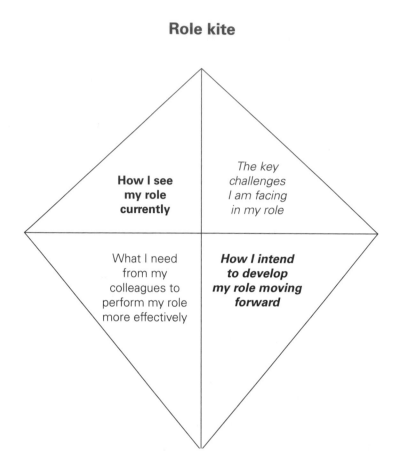

How I see
my role
currently

*The key
challenges
I am facing
in my role*

What I need
from my
colleagues to
perform my role
more effectively

***How I intend
to develop
my role moving
forward***

As you can see on the illustration, the kite has four sections and in each of these, team members must write a few words responding to the appropriate heading. I usually get people to construct their role kite on a large piece of flipchart paper. Then, when everyone has completed their kite, I simply invite each team member to stand by the chart and talk everyone else through what they have written and why. The exercise is always successful in generating really interesting and productive discussion during which team members begin to coach each other around the challenges they are facing in their respective roles. Once this starts to happen then steps are being taken towards the creation of a winning environment. So, Basil, it may sound obvious but creating conversations among team members about roles is fundamental to a leader's role and will inevitably contribute positively to the development of mental toughness. Think about how you could get your team to engage in an exercise like this so that you can become totally confident in your role functioning.

Quick Win 2: Play to strengths

It's important that players accept their responsibility without becoming burdened by it. I've always been quite analytical. I try to quickly identify a player's strengths. I encourage them, I emphasize the 'dos' rather than the 'don'ts'. Some coaches impose themselves too much on individual players. I just try to create the environment within which they can flourish.[2]

John Inverarity, former coach of the Warwickshire Bears Cricket Team

It is logical to assume that if you wish to focus on performing well under pressure and making confident decisions around choices and risk, then you will be far more successful if you utilize your strengths as a platform. Nevertheless, obvious as it sounds, it is amazing how often people lose sight of their strengths at the very time they need to be focusing on them the most! What are you really good at? What skills and attributes have got you to where you are today? What can you totally rely on in yourself when the heat is on? What sort of things are you great at when you get into the 'zone' or go onto 'autopilot'? The answers to these, and similar questions, should point you towards your strengths and, in so doing, significantly help you make choices about your actions and behaviour. I believe that leaders have a responsibility to encourage and facilitate this thinking process in the way that John Inverarity suggests in his quote.

In their book *Now Discover Your Strengths*, Marcus Bucking-ham and Donald Clifton outline their philosophy of facilitating high achievement by helping people identify exactly what their strengths are and then advising them to find ways of practis-ing and refining those strengths. The approach has been well received and it seems entirely logical to suggest that a strengths orientation focus will contribute to the creation of a winning environment and the demonstration of the three elements at the heart of my mental toughness model – i.e. self-belief, clear thinking and resilience.

> *When Brian Clough first came to Nottingham Forest, everyone at that time picked on all the things that I couldn't do – I couldn't tackle, I couldn't head, I wasn't the quickest person – but it didn't seem to worry him at all and he concentrated on things that I was good at.*[3]

John Robertson, former Scottish footballer

John Robertson played for Nottingham Forest when they were at the peak of their success under Brian Clough. His quote about Clough's management approach would, I strongly believe, be heartily supported by Marcus Buckingham and Donald Clifton. Imagine you were in Robertson's position when Clough arrived and think how your mindset and attitude towards pressure, challenge and risk would have changed under the new regime. You would undoubtedly feel more confident to try new things, to take up challenges and expose yourself to risky options – knowing that your manager was supporting you and focusing on what you were good at.

Once again, you may not have a boss who does this well and so you will need to take responsibility for yourself. Consider how you can pay attention to your strengths and be aware of how they work for you. Avoid being too modest about these strengths but instead use your awareness of them to develop more robust confidence. We all have talents but it is astonishing how some people lack basic awareness of what these talents are. Consider how you could spend some time reflecting on what you consider your five 'signature strengths' to be. These represent the things that you really excel at. Things that you know you can rely on in yourself. Attributes and talents that people readily recognize in you as adding significant value to your team or organization. Reflecting on these signature strengths and completing the table below (which also asks you to consider how you might use your strengths more effectively) will again, contribute to the creation of your own winning environment.

If you find this particularly difficult, it is useful to get some feedback from colleagues, friends and even family. Talk to them about what they see as your fundamental strengths and how valuable they are to the organization. Ask for their views on how you could start to utilize these strengths more and/or differently. Conversations like this will raise your self-awareness and hence your capacity to focus on your strengths when facing tough situations.

Signature strength	How I could use it more effectively
1.	
2.	
3.	
4.	
5.	

The next table shows a real example of a signature strength chart. Kate was an HR manager who I coached through a very turbulent time in the life of her organization. She did not have a very supportive boss and had to rely on her own techniques for creating a winning environment. She found the task of completing this chart extremely helpful as a coping strategy.

Signature strength	How I could use it more effectively
1. I'm *great with people* – I know that I can build relationships easily and people seem to place high levels of trust in me	Access these relationships more often – I need to be better at 'asking' for help sometimes. People won't be irritated. They will actually be happy to offer me some support
2. My *mental stamina* – I can concentrate on my own for long periods and get closure on things even when I'm really tired	I think it would help if I could find a couple of times each week when I lock myself away in a meeting room down the corridor from my regular work space. I could achieve an enormous amount in just a couple of hours without interruptions which would set me up for the rest of the week
3. My *organization skills* – everyone tells me how organized I am and this allows me to juggle lots of different things at once	Spend less time worrying when things are going wrong and the pressure is on – divert my efforts into organizing. I know that I derive satisfaction from being organized and it helps me cope with pressure so make sure that I access this skill as much as possible
4. My *sense of humour* – I'm good at keeping people amused in stressful times and can always find the lighter side to things	Use my humour with 'me' more – instead of making everyone else laugh quite so much, utilize the humour to help lighten my own stresses and pressure
5. *Seeing the big picture* – I find it easy to stand back and reflect on how things fit together. People compliment me on my ability to visualize the future	When I'm under stress, I must consciously take a step back and recognize that the pressure is temporary and that in the wider scheme of things, the current pressure is not that significant

Quick Win 3: Enjoy the ride

The most important thing of the lot though, is to turn up with a smile on your face, whether for training, practice or play. There's enough pressure as it is. My aim is to take the pressure off, to encourage the players to relax and be themselves. I want everyone to enjoy their cricket and if they do, a better performance will come from it.[4]

Michael Vaughan, captain of the 2005 Ashes winning England Cricket Team

Michael Vaughan's leadership style has enjoyment at its heart. I have listened to some of his team talks over the years and it is rare for him to finish one without making reference to the importance of enjoyment. This was certainly a theme throughout the 2005 Ashes series. Yes it was going to be a massive challenge with lots of ups and downs and twists and turns. Yes there would be periods of real pressure and intensity. The media distractions would inevitably be intrusive and irritating. The expectation from spectators and fans would heighten the stress. The series would be physically, mentally and emotionally draining. But … it was going to be essential that the team enjoyed the ride and had fun along the way. Even as the series drew to its cliffhanging conclusion in the early days of September, Vaughan reinforced his mantra as the players stepped across the white line and into the great white heat of the final stages of the battle.

This is what we have prepared for. This is what we have waited for. Enjoy it.[5]

Michael Vaughan, captain of the 2005 Ashes winning England Cricket Team

When people are enjoying themselves it's so much easier to feel confident and relaxed. The absence of fear is such a great antidote to the debilitating effects of pressure. Working with others in an environment which values fun and enjoyment creates the kind of 'vapour' that is conducive to people going the extra mile and staying committed even when the odds are against them.

There is even medical evidence to support the view that laughter can positively influence our health. It has been shown that laughter reduces our cortisol levels (the stress hormone that I discussed earlier in the book) and can also benefit the immune system by increasing the number and activity of Killer T cells which help the body fight against viral attacks and damaged cells. So making the effort to engage in activities that make you laugh or being around people and things that you find amusing should be part of your game plan for creating a winning environment.

Enjoying the moment is something that comes more naturally to some than others. If you find it difficult to absorb yourself in the present and simply enjoy it for its own sake then you may need to engage in some self-coaching. When you sense yourself getting overwhelmed, remind yourself that performance should be fun and that even if you have a miserable boss who is incapable of seeing the funny side of things, you are in control of your attitudes and thoughts. Your attitude is your decision and no one else's. Look out for every opportunity to make things enjoyable and keep a smile on your face whenever you can. If you can do this you'll have contributed another essential element in the creation of your own winning environment.

In the old days of professional sport there was an adage that was well used in locker rooms up and down the country – 'win or lose let's get on the booze'. Due to the profound changes in standards within sport this adage does not get used any more within successful teams who, thankfully, have a far more professional approach to their performance due to the contributions of sports science in recent years. Although not quite as catchy, my suggestion for a new adage would be something like 'win or lose, enjoy the battle'. Regardless of the outcome it should still be possible to enjoy the process. Stiff competition, performing under intense pressure, working to hit a challenging deadline can all be enjoyable processes if you think and focus in the right way. Don't let your enjoyment be dictated solely by the outcome. Enjoy things along the way and as the great tennis player Arthur Ashe once said, 'Success is a journey not a destination. The doing is often more important than the outcome.'

A final thought ...

An inevitable feature of a winning environment is the constant focus on raising the bar and taking performance to the next level. In very simple terms the well-established *stop, start, continue* technique is a useful way of maintaining this mindset. It is particularly useful if you are in some sort of leadership position because you will then be responsible for helping others create their winning environments as well as your own.

The way this technique works is very straightforward and it is often used in 360 assessment processes due to the combined power of its simplicity and capacity to generate impactful data. In the current context I would use the task of completing the following three statements to guide a planning process around specific actions that could be taken to positively affect the nature of the current environment:

- 'In order for me to create a better winning environment and hence take performance to the next level, I should *stop*...'
- 'In order for me to create a better winning environment and hence take performance to the next level, I should *start*...'
- 'In order for me to create a better winning environment and hence take performance to the next level, I should *continue*...'

The way in which these statements can be considered can vary but it's often worth involving someone else in your thinking so that you can bounce ideas around and be challenged to fully evaluate your thoughts.

The chart opposite reflects the output from a coaching session I conducted with a supermarket store manager a while ago. Neil was becoming increasingly conscious of the fact that the environment around his team was not as he wanted but was struggling to put any structure to his thinking regarding an action plan. I suggested we use the *stop, start, continue* approach and it helped him clarify his thoughts quite quickly. You'll see the wide range of actions within his chart but each of them would, in some small way, contribute to creating a winning environment.

Neil's 'Winning Environment' Strategy

STOP	START	CONTINUE
• Being quite so HANDS ON – this goes for the top team as well as myself	• Slowly extending the warehouse meetings – more frequent and at different times with more note taking	• Feedback process with top team and extended to Controllers

• Accepting/tolerating poor performance
So I need to:
  ○ Set better standards/goals
  ○ Reduce knowledge/skills gap
  ○ Communicate gaps to them
	• Innovating re: incentives (DVD ideas)
	  ○ Individualized
	  ○ Need to do necessary analysis re: targets/goals/performance review
	  ○ Demonstrate/celebrate successes among the team
		• Good communication systems like the warehouse meetings

• Accepting that broken equipment cannot get fixed quickly
So I need to:
  ○ Get orders/requests in
  ○ Get time scales
  ○ Follow-up
  ○ Get more ruthless
  ○ Speak directly to bosses
	• More team events for the staff such as quiz nights/outings etc.
	  ○ Set up a committee for idea generation
	  ○ Find the resources
	  ○ Communicate to everyone
	  ○ Top team support/attendance
		• Positive approach to people management
		  ○ Hellos
		  ○ Thank yous
		  ○ Well dones
		  ○ Smiling approach
		  ○ Seek out motivational feedback opportunities

	• Community links
	  ○ Involve Regional Manager
	  ○ Get our product into their world
		• Deliverance of challenges to the team
		  ○ Short term goals/successes
		  ○ The fresh fruit campaign

		• Analysing performance
		  ○ Taking time out
		  ○ The finite detail
		  ○ Push harder to achieve results

		• Challenging myself to have 'adult to adult' interactions

In conclusion, there is no doubting the role that the environment plays in fostering a winning approach to mental toughness. It doesn't matter how talented someone is, if they are not operating within the right kind of environment they will struggle to deliver anywhere near their potential. It is clearly the role of the business leader to create this environment but if they are not doing so then all is not lost – seek to create your own. There are certain things that you can control – both inside your head and in relation to the dynamics of the environment. Figure these out as quickly as you can and then focus on influencing them positively. You may be surprised at the effect on your overall mental toughness having created your own winning environment.

The Game Plan for Creating your Winning Environment

- Make sure that you fully understand your role and are happy with your capacity to execute it. Be proactive in initiating conversations with your boss and colleagues about role functioning.

- Spend time reflecting on your signature strengths and consider how you can use them more effectively.

- Be sure to enjoy the challenges. Keep smiling and laugh whenever you can.

- Conduct a *stop, start, continue* exercise periodically as a way of identifying a broad range of actions that will impact on others as well as yourself.

Perspectives from the Front Line

8

Robin Mills is the HR Director for the Woolworths Group plc which is one of the UK's leading retailers focusing on 'kids, celebrations and the home'. The company employs 30,000 people and serves around six million customers per week throughout 822 stores up and down the country. Robin's job is fast-paced, dynamic and requires high levels of mental toughness to enable him to manage his own pressures as well as coaching others.

I have worked with Robin for several years now and I have always felt that he is a mentally tough performer who handles pressure well and consequently has had an extremely successful career resulting in his appointment to his current role of Group HR Director at the age of 36. Returning to my mental toughness model and the three elements within the central box – Robin demonstrates strong and robust self-belief, he thinks very clearly (especially in pressure situations) and he is exceedingly resilient. Throughout his career he has had to deal with some very tough environments such as significant organizational change interventions, pay negotiations and redundancy programmes. He has endured incredibly long working hours which have tested his commitment to maintaining a good work–life balance. I have been continually impressed by Robin's ability to manage his attitude and approach at work with his commitment as a husband and father of four children under the age of ten! For these reasons, I invited Robin to be a part of this book and he agreed to me picking his brain about his personal perspectives on developing a winning approach to mental toughness in business.

Although we have had many conversations over the years about sport, business, winning and mental toughness I felt it would be interesting to take stock of Robin's latest thinking and capture his ideas in terms of how they relate to the content of this book. So we met at a hotel just outside London during April of 2006 and spent the afternoon drinking tea and exploring Robin's personal perspectives from the 'front line'. Here's a summary of the conversation with parts of the content reproduced in Robin's own words. As you read the narrative, you will note that reference is made to each of the ten tips contained within my mental toughness model.

Robin opened the conversation with his main point which was that virtually everything in his mind comes back to the challenge of reframing.

> *RM: The biggest theme which resonates with me is the 'reframing' approach. A lot of what it boils down to and a lot of my own mental toughness is down to a constructive approach to reframing. I have a rule that says sometimes you can't change things but you can change how you think about them. You can change what they mean and it's all about what things mean. So when the going gets tough and when the numbers are disappointing it's about coaching people to see things in the most helpful way that they can – the most helpful*

way to mobilize them into action. So the dimension that matters is not whether something is good or bad or right or wrong but whether it is helpful or unhelpful. This is a dimension that sits with me constantly. What is the most helpful thing to do here?

This clearly relates strongly to Tip 9: 'Reframe your appraisal' although as the discussion ensued Robin felt that the skill cut across other areas in the model as well. His basic view was that managing appraisal was at the heart of mental toughness as far as he was concerned. He then broadened his thinking to consider the importance of reframing for business leaders.

RM: I think the reframing thing is the single best tool that business leaders have for themselves and for others. At the end of the day it's all about how you see things that enables you either to move to action or not move to action.

I went on to ask Robin how easy he found this and whether he felt he had improved over time.

RM: I am a naturally optimistic person so I guess it may come easier to me than others but I have definitely got better at it over the years. When I'm trying to keep myself healthy and mentally tough I examine closely how I am thinking about things. You have to work at this – you have to take conscious steps. You have to work at catching yourself. Sometimes you can give yourself a break and wallow a little but sooner or later you've got to sit up and do something positive. You need to take control of the situation and decide what exactly is going to the most helpful course of action. Dealing with unionized warehouses is a tough environment and mental tough-

ness is essential – wage negotiations with stewards are generally difficult and uncomfortable situations. You can only survive on what is inside you and a key part of this is your capacity to reframe and think differently about the challenges you're facing.

I have consulted in several major retail organizations in recent years. In these companies, the senior executives are constantly analysing numbers. They are particularly interested in what they refer to as 'like for like sales'. In other words, as an example, how do this week's figures compare with the corresponding week last year. All other things being equal have we improved our sales? We spoke at length about the Monday meetings in which the previous week's numbers are examined.

RM: If I think about a disappointing set of numbers on a Monday and I start to think about what the implications are for me and my life it's really important for me to consider this in the wider context of my life – it's about keeping a balanced perspective. The big question about bad numbers is 'what do they mean?' Is it a market issue, is it a store issue, is it something we've done or not done. So it's not about whether we've lost or if we've failed – it's about problem solving, understanding exactly what's happening and then doing something about it.

You will recall that keeping perspective was an integral part of Tip 7: 'Manage your outlook'. This is a key technique that Robin uses to help him with deal with disappointing business results and thus avoid the temptation of slipping into the pitfalls of crooked thinking.

Robin relates strongly to the idea of 'clutch moments'. He maintains that mentally tough individuals can recognize these clutch moments and hence work hard to create time and space to think ahead.

> *RM: You've got to recognize the clutch situations and work hard to create time and space to think ahead. Mentally tough people don't get caught in the middle of a clutch moment. They figure out very quickly what are the really important things. When a crisis moment emerges, I am comfortable just 'holding' it in the minute – I see others itching to move to immediate action which may be premature. I am able to stay calm and focused enabling me to make the right decision. You need to be mentally strong to hold on in those situations and avoid jumping in to a decision or action too early.*

These comments of course relate to Critical Moment Toughness and you will remember the comments I made about slowing down when faced with certain pressure situations. Recall the comments by Nasser Hussain about the feedback he received regarding his general demeanour as compared with that of Michael Atherton. Robin speaks a lot about the importance of being cool. It's a word that clearly resonates with him.

> *RM: You've got to be cool with yourself. You cannot go around like a headless chicken shouting in a high-pitched voice. I often say to my team, 'Right this is going to be tough. We've got a plan of action and it's going to be good but we've got to be cool'. You've also got to get cool with the way things are. I don't try and take on what I see as the lay of the land. I very quickly accept*

the situation as it is and acknowledge the rules of the game. This doesn't mean I don't try to change things when possible. It's back to your adage of 'control the controllables'. You cannot waste energy and effort on the uncontrollables – they will wear you out. Stay in the zone of the things that you can have an effect on.

The effects of this 'cool' approach will have the added advantage of helping to manage energy (Tip 6). If you're not able to remain calm and in control then you will very quickly become tired, which will have an adverse effect on your decision making and, over time, will result in fatigue and exhaustion. This is precisely why so many people do not cope well with stress and pressure. They burn up so much energy by rushing around and being overly emotional. Robin's advice? – stay cool and in control and you'll be well on the way to managing the situation as well as your own energy. Tip 4: 'Control the controllables' is ever present in Robin's mind and it is something that he actively seeks to coach in his direct reports.

Robin feels that the environment in which you are working will contribute to your capacity to 'stay cool'. He is a big fan of people clubbing together to create an environment (Tip 10) which is conducive to being cool in the face of severe challenge and pressure.

RM: When I worked in a previous organization, I was involved in implementing change under extremely challenging circumstances. It was a very tough environment in which we had to have a very clear purpose and then stick steadfastly to the line we had agreed. We were able to do this by creating a very supportive environment. We worked together and created an environment which was conducive to delivering optimal per-

*formance under conditions of relentless pressure. Part
of this is also about having a confidant – someone you
can speak with about the difficulties you are facing.
You cannot do it all yourself. You've got to have some
support. But you must be quite careful in who you select
for this type of support and these conversations. I always
try to avoid 'mood hoovers' – people who sap energy
from the environment. You refer to them as 'negahol-
ics'. They just don't help. I have a close colleague who is
the opposite to this. We have great conversations and he
acts as an excellent sounding board knowing when to
challenge me and when to be appropriately supportive.
If we have had a disappointing week, he will give me
some serious comment for five minutes and then will
bring humour into the situation and help me move on.
Again it's back to the 'helpful vs. not helpful' thing.*

Robin loves the challenge and is a superb role model for Tip
8: 'Seek out the challenge'. He recognizes it in himself and is
always on the lookout for it in others.

*RM: I love the attitude of 'bring it on'. If someone chooses
to get adversarial with me I rarely avoid the conflict. I
will actively confront the issue. I do not hide from con-
frontation. I back myself to deal with the situation positively and I will stick with it until the issue is resolved
and goes away. This requires toughness and is essential
in the tough environment in which I am used to working. I enjoy this process. It's not easy but it adds zest and
spice to my job.*

He expands this point by using one of his favourite phrases
– 'facing into it'. By this he means loving the challenge of facing
something really difficult. It's the opposite of being intimidated

and threatened by a demanding situation. He speaks of viewing a challenge as an 'opportunity' to show yourself rather than
worrying about the threat of being exposed or failing to cope.

> *RM: I enjoy facing into it. It's a matter of saying 'what
> have we got here?'. Then dusting it off, stripping it down
> and putting it in front of the group, or yourself, and
> teeing it up as an opportunity. OK, now we know what
> it is – let's do a really good job of sorting it out. Yes it's
> tough, but I love it. Come on – bring it on.*

Then what about when things don't go as you intend, I asked
him. His response immediately connected with Tip 3: 'Learn
and move on'.

> *RM: You've got to be able to take meaning from what
> has happened in order to drive further action. You've
> got to move on quickly because generally mental tough-
> ness is about bad things. It may be an old cliché, but it
> really is true … today's newspaper will be tomorrow's
> chip paper. You cannot dwell on things. You've got to
> move on. Again it's a reframing thing. Learn from the
> situation, identify what you're going to do and move
> on. Leave it behind you.*

He then went on to connect this mindset to the challenges of
taking risks.

> *RM: Risk taking is a big part of retail. You have to take
> some big punts without necessarily having the data.
> People who are good at this remember their successes.
> It's almost comical how good they are at remembering
> their achievements and conveniently forgetting their
> failures. They also keep things in perspective. It's not*

the end of the world. They downplay the failures. They don't see it as a risk. They see it as why they're there. That's what they're paid for. It's simply what they do as opposed to consciously taking a risk as such.

This presents another version of Tip 2: 'Reconnect with previous successes'. Mentally tough individuals are really good at staying connected with their achievements and tend to play down their failures by, once again, keeping things in perspective. Robin then went on to expand this point by discussing strengths and self-awareness.

RM: I'm a fan of the 'spikes of strengths' way of thinking as opposed to people being generally good at lots of things. I am more tuned in these days to helping people maximize their spikes and manage their gaps. I don't try to turn people into something they're never going to be. You need to be totally tuned in to where your strengths lie and make sure that you are making the most of them whenever you can. To do this effectively, you have to have high levels of self-awareness. Really knowing yourself is part of the make-up. As I've learnt about myself over the years, I know how to get the best out of myself. I know what to take on and what to avoid. Being frank and honest with yourself is crucial. This helps so much when the going gets tough.

This connects nicely into the points I was making earlier in the book when I outlined the processes of actively seeking out feedback and identifying your signature strengths. Both of these processes are a fundamental part of developing self-awareness and when done well will help you to become totally comfortable with who you are and what you're really good at. Robin went on to explain how this will allow you to approach

situations with a real feeling of confidence by being absolutely
true to yourself.

> *RM: I am a big fan of 'if you're not being yourself then
> it creates stress'. If you can't find a way of being who
> you are and being absolutely true to this and find a
> way of liking yourself, being proud of what you do and
> the way you treat people then you can't be mentally
> tough. You've got to be proud of the way you approach
> your work. You've got to be prepared to put your name
> to stuff. If you find yourself bending all over the place
> – I think you'll be unhappy. You've got to find a way of
> being who you are. As you get more senior also you've
> got to start being prepared to give more of yourself away.
> In the retail world, you are on your feet quite a lot and
> in front of groups of people a lot. You have big teams
> working for you. People really want to know who you
> are and you must be confident enough to tell them.*

Tip 5: 'See and think success' is a vital part of this process. It's
going to be difficult to enter a stressful situation with confidence and imagining success if you are unsure of who you are
and what you should be doing to come across as truly authen-
tic. If you are very self-aware you will find it so much easier to
positively see and think yourself into a performance.

Robin identifies a linking element between self-awareness and
keeping perspective. He relates strongly to the term 'grounding' which refers to getting in touch with your senses and being
calm and in control of yourself irrespective of the stresses you
may be experiencing. The term bears many similarities with my
highlights section within Tip 7: 'Manage your outlook'.

RM: I really like the grounding thing. Steve, you talk about being in the countryside with your dog. I relate to the concept of feeling your feet in your shoes and that whole thing about being centred. When you are more grounded you tend to be more open to what's going on around you. You can see the leaves on the trees but also you can read people better and understand the meanings in things. Again it's about being cool. It's also about growing. You have to keep growing but in order to do so you must be grounded. Growing is very much part of the grounding process. You must be open to listen. Stay in the moment when it hurts. This is all based on being grounded. I got a quote once from a book called Manifest Your Destiny *by Wayne Dyer which I really like: 'Life is like a dance. The point is not to get from A to B. The point is to enjoy every step along the way'. That's my thing. Even when they're shouting at you. Even when the numbers are disappointing and things seem to be falling apart, you've got to be open enough to take something from it, to listen to it, to enjoy something in the situation.*

The one remaining tip which has not been referenced yet is Tip 1: 'Adopt an athlete mindset'. Robin saved this until last and he made his point strongly.

RM: People now recognize the importance of mental preparation much more than they did five or ten years ago. This is well proven. We all know it works. The idea of looking after your mind is properly understood by senior people in business. So the question is, how serious about this will your reader be? They've picked up the book so must have some ambition. But they must ask themselves whether what they're doing actually matches

> *that ambition. The book is most definitely about making yourself mentally tough and being successful in business. But what exactly are they going to do?*

This is an excellent point that Robin makes. The role of the mind in performance is not a speculative thing any more – if indeed it ever was. It is well proven and cannot be ignored. So you really need to ask yourself how committed you are to doing something about it. Remember the athlete mindset is all about challenging yourself to raise your performance bar. It's about mentally preparing for performance challenges and engaging in quality review thinking afterwards to ensure learning has taken place. Robin explains that he is constantly on the lookout for evidence of this type of mindset in employees and that those that display it are well aware of how they should be thinking and behaving in order to take themselves to the next level.

> *RM: I like to spot junior people in the organization who look like they should be in a senior position already. If you're a store manager who wants to be a regional manager then you should think, behave and look like a regional manager. Play the part right now. It's not about being perfect though. In fact, when I was appointed to become an HR Director one of the best pieces of advice I was given was that I did not have to be the finished article straightaway. It was OK to look like I was learning. I didn't have to be the perfect HR Director two weeks after being appointed. But I did have to look like I was committed and focused on getting better and better in the role. I had to adopt an 'athlete mindset' and in doing so I was able to deliver some strong performances in the early days which set me up for further growth and development.*

To conclude then, this conversation with Robin has touched on all ten tips and hence connected coherently with my mental toughness model and the various components within it. The final challenge from Robin about what you are actually going to do is a perfect introduction to the book's final chapter which will help you convert what you have read and digested into a meaningful set of actions to form your game plan. I hope you enjoyed reading about Robin's thoughts and ideas and that perhaps they have given you a greater understanding of what a winning approach to mental toughness looks like from someone who is most definitely performing on the front line.

Finalizing your Game Plan

I hope you've found this book to be an interesting read and have enjoyed the stories and anecdotes that I have woven into the text. However, it's now important that you take some time to really start to formalize your game plan and identify exactly what you're going to do as a result of the ideas that have been presented. This will involve reflecting on the actions that arise from each of the sections and specifically from the 10 tips that form part of the mental toughness model – a complete version of which is shown overleaf.

Before challenging you to create your actions though, it's worth pausing and reflecting on how you would rate yourself currently on each of the elements within the model. A good way of doing this is to use a technique called performance profiling which is commonly used in sport and which I, and others, have used successfully in business too. The technique was pioneered by Professor Lew Hardy and Dr Richard Butler in the mid 1990s and has been embraced by many Olympic athletes ever since. It's a simple technique that requires you to rate yourself on certain performance dimensions at the beginning of an intervention programme and then again at a later date. There are various ways of illustrating the scores but a popular

Mental toughness model
'Creating the game plan'

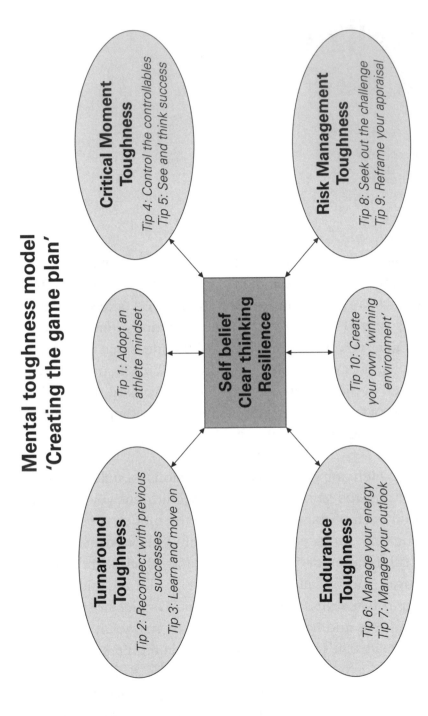

one is as a wagon wheel with each wheel section representing one of the performance dimensions.

As you will see from the profile overleaf, I'm asking you to use a seven point scale to assess your relative strength in each of the ten tips. Here is a guide as to how you can apply the seven points.

7   ***Exceptional***. I am incredibly strong in this aspect and can implement the skills involved without having to concentrate on them. I could confidently coach someone else in every aspect of this tip.

6   ***Really strong***. This is definitely one of my best areas and there's only a little bit more I need to do before I nail it. I'm almost there.

5   ***Good***. I'm aware of how well this tip can work for me and I use it quite a lot. There is room for improvement though and I need to think about how I can raise the bar and use the tip more effectively.

4   ***OK***. I'm all right at this but I couldn't call it a strength. There's a lot more I can do to become better at using it to my advantage and I need to start changing right away.

3   ***Below par***. Although I understand the importance of this tip I rarely implement it in a way that impacts on my performance. I should prioritize this in my action plan and get working at it straightaway.

2   ***Not even close***. I'm really a long way from using this tip at all. I know that it's important but it just doesn't seem to feature in my everyday thoughts.

1   ***Off the radar***. Before reading this book, it would never have occurred to me to do this. I'm starting from the absolute bottom of the ladder and need to get climbing quickly.

Using this scale as a guide, I'd now like you to consider what ratings you would currently give yourself for each of the

Mental toughness profile

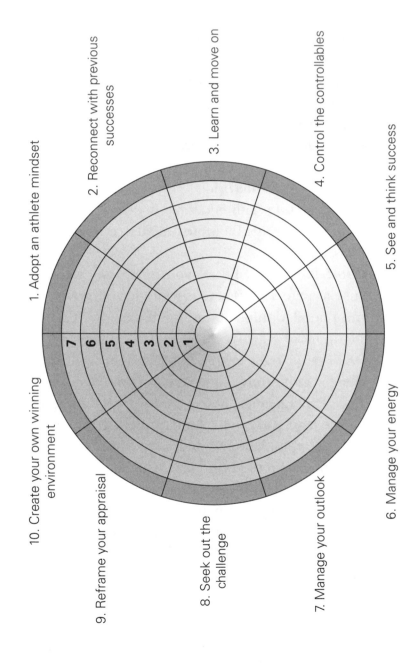

1. Adopt an athlete mindset

2. Reconnect with previous successes

3. Learn and move on

4. Control the controllables

5. See and think success

6. Manage your energy

7. Manage your outlook

8. Seek out the challenge

9. Reframe your appraisal

10. Create your own winning environment

dimensions. When you've decided, shade in the appropriate area of the wagon wheel profile and see what kind of pattern emerges. To use the wagon wheel metaphor, imagine how smooth your ride would be if you had shaded all 7s to make a perfect circle as compared to the bumpy ride that other patterns would result in. Here are some reminder notes to assist you in allocating scores.

- *Tip 1: Adopt an athlete mindset*. How well do you prepare for your performance challenges? How well do you engage in quality review processes? To what extent are you constantly on the lookout for ways in which you can improve your mental game and hence raise your performance bar?

- *Tip 2: Reconnect with previous successes*. How good are you at staying connected with your previous accomplishments especially when things are not going so well for you? How quickly could you identify meaningful achievements you have stored across different areas of your life?

- *Tip 3: Learn and move on*. How well do you learn and move on as opposed to getting bogged down in the frustrations and disappointments of what has passed? Do you have mental plans to help you do this?

- *Tip 4: Control the controllables*. How well do you focus your energy and efforts on the controllables? How well do you maintain a process focus during challenging times and to what extent are you absolutely clear how your process goals contribute to what you are wanting to achieve?

- *Tip 5: See and think success*. How often do you find yourself engaging in 'don't' thinking? How well do you use visualization as a means of preparing yourself for difficult situations? How good are you at calming down and moving more slowly when the heat is on and you're feeling anxious?

- ***Tip 6: Manage your energy***. Does your level of physical activity help or hinder your well-being and overall health? Do you try to incorporate some sort of physical activity into your daily schedule? How good is your diet? Are you managing your diet in a way that will boost your immune system and give you sustained energy throughout long working days? How well do you relax? Are you actively taking steps to reduce the cortisol levels in your system?

- ***Tip 7: Manage your outlook***. How optimistic a person are you? How good are you at focusing on highlights in your life, however small they may be? Are you able to maintain perspective even when things are really tough? Overall, are you a positive person who *brings* energy to a team or a negaholic who *takes* energy away?

- ***Tip 8: Seek out the challenge***. How good are you at demonstrating a 'challenge seeking' attitude? Are you hungry for feedback and how much do you actively seek it from your boss, colleagues and reports as a way of improving your performance?

- ***Tip 9: Reframe your appraisal***. How good are you at reframing the way you appraise situations as a way of giving you more confidence? How often do find yourself slipping into crooked thinking?

- ***Tip 10: Create your own winning environment***. To what extent are you absolutely clear about your role at work? Are you comfortable with this role? How clear are you on your signature strengths and how well do you utilize them? How good are you at enjoying the moment and loving the challenges that you face at work? Do you have a technique like the *stop, start, continue* process to ensure that you are constantly looking to develop your winning environment?

Now that you have your shaded wagon wheel you should have a feel for where your priorities are in developing your game plan. At this point it's also a good idea to set some goals around the scores that you currently have. For example, over the next 3–6 months, what kind of improvement could you aim for in each of the areas? When you've thought about this, go back to the wagon wheel and put a coloured mark against the line representing your target score.

Now it's time to formulate and finalize your game plan. This will involve revisiting and rereading each section of the book with a real focus on considering what your key takeaways and actions will be. You can do this in any order according to the shape of your wagon wheel. There is no correct way to do this and there are no rules pertaining to time frames either. I just want to encourage you to clearly identify what practical things are going to constitute your game plan so that the book becomes a really useful tool rather than an interesting read which gets put back on the shelf and not acted upon.

Tony's story

A couple of days before writing this chapter I spent a day working with Tony Holmes and his executive team. Tony is the Wholesale Director for Coca-Cola Enterprises in the UK and I began coaching him around four years ago. He is an action-orientated kind of guy, very high in energy and enthusiasm and extremely well respected by the people who work for him. Over the years of our coaching relationship we have covered a huge amount of material and ideas relating to personal and performance development. As a way of co-ordinating all his thoughts and actions from the sessions that we have, he uses an A5 sized notebook in which he records the following three things: (i) notes from our discussions; (ii) books and articles that he wants to read to expand his knowledge; (iii) his action plans. The notebook does not have a prescribed structure as such but it is a convenient way of him keeping all his thoughts and information relating to performance development in one place. He *always* brings the notebook to 1–1 coaching sessions as well as team development events like the one we had this week. He also provides all those who report to him directly with such a notebook and when presenting them with it, he does not tell them how to use it. He merely encourages them to use it in a way that will work for them. I really like this approach to action planning. In my experience, preferred style and format for action planning varies enormously between different people. Attempting to prescribe to people a set way of recording their plans does not work. So I'm simply going to encourage you in the way Tony does with his team. Invest in a notebook which you designate as your game plan log. It might even be an electronic notebook in the form of a special folder on your laptop or handheld computer. It really doesn't matter as long as you have something. This is Tony's point to his team. Use whatever method works for you but just make sure you are capturing your goals and actions in some sort of written form so that you can monitor your progress over time.

The process

Having completed the mental toughness wagon wheel profile and decided on whether you intend to buy a notebook or create an electronic version you are in a position to begin constructing your game plan. Your wagon wheel will give you an idea of where your priorities lie so you may wish to construct the order of the plan according to your ratings. Alternatively, you could simply construct a plan in relation to the order in which the ten tips are presented in the book – i.e. starting with 'adopt an athlete mindset' and finishing with 'create your own winning environment'. Either way, you will need to reread the appropriate sections of the book and then use the action charts at the end of each chapter to help you choose your specific actions. The checklist chart opposite will help you track your progress in constructing your game plan as well as guiding you to the appropriate pages for each of the ten tips. It requires you to tick a box when you have reread the appropriate section,

MY GAME PLAN CHECKLIST

10 mental toughness tips	Section re-read (tick box)	Action plan recorded (tick box)	Comments (tick box)
To begin… Tip 1: Adopt an athlete mindset (p. 24)	☐	☐	
Turnaround Toughness			
Tip 2: Reconnect with previous successes (p. 33)	☐	☐	
Tip 3: Learn and move on (p. 43)	☐	☐	
Critical Moment Toughness			
Tip 4: Control the controllables (p. 51)	☐	☐	
Tip 5: See and think success (p. 62)	☐	☐	
Endurance Toughness			
Tip 6: Manage your energy (p. 77)	☐	☐	
Tip 7: Manage your outlook (p. 97)	☐	☐	
Risk Management Toughness			
Tip 8: Seek out the challenge (p. 118)	☐	☐	
Tip 9: Reframe your appraisal (p. 129)	☐	☐	
To conclude… Tip 10: Create your own winning environment (p. 145)	☐	☐	

another when you have devised your action plan and then add some comments in the final column along with an intended date for review and evaluation of progress.

You can start working on your plan as soon as you begin to create it – don't wait until it's completed to get going. There should be little things that you can implement immediately which will start to give you some momentum as you develop your winning approach to mental toughness. It's worth also thinking about who you might wish to discuss your plan with. A different perspective is always useful in any action planning process and another person is often able to help you identify strategies for overcoming some of the barriers and obstacles you may encounter in putting your game plan in place. Bouncing ideas off someone you trust and respect is definitely worth considering.

So the planning process can be summarized in these six steps:

Step 1 Complete the mental toughness wagon wheel profile.

Step 2 Decide on your preferred means of recording your game plan notes.

Step 3 Reread the appropriate sections of the book and construct a personalized game plan set of actions and goals.

Step 4 Complete the game plan checklist sheet, identifying when you will review each section of the plan.

Step 5 Execute the plan over the coming weeks and months.

Step 6 In 3–6 months, review and evaluate your progress and complete a new mental toughness wagon wheel profile.

Practise being a game plan coach
Now that you have your own game plan and you're an expert in all the various dimensions of mental toughness, I'm going to

challenge you to reflect on how you might coach and advise the four individuals described in Chapter 2. You will recall that I originally presented a mental toughness scenario for each of the four dimensions in my model. Let's review each of them and you can think about what specific advice you feel is appropriate for each individual given their particular situation. As well as being a bit of fun, this will help you to further embed your learnings from the ten tips.

The first scenario was Geoff who was in need of some coaching on Turnaround Toughness.

Mental Toughness Scenario 1: Geoff – 35-year-old marketing manager

Geoff is a confident guy who has had many successes during his time working in three different organizations over the past 12 years. However, the team that he manages has failed to deliver against its targets this year and Geoff is feeling responsible for the disappointing performance. Added to this, he has recently received a poor performance appraisal from his boss which ranked as the worst he has ever had. He is feeling very down about the current situation and is aware that his confidence has taken a beating. He and his team have a tough time coming up in the next few months and he knows that he will need to be resilient and tough to deal with all the impending pressures that are inevitable. But he can't seem to get positive about things and he is struggling to regain his usual confidence. Each day seems to present another potential disappointment and Geoff knows that he must break this cycle of negativity in which he finds himself.

So consider which aspects of the two Turnaround Toughness tips might be appropriate and helpful for Geoff in his quest to break his cycle of negativity. Make some notes in the blank chart below.

My advice to Geoff

Next was Laura, the sales executive who needed a strong dose of critical moment toughness.

Mental Toughness Scenario 2: Laura – 28-year-old sales executive

Laura is a talented salesperson who regularly exceeds her annual targets. She is a confident extrovert who loves the challenge of influencing customers and closing deals. Her interpersonal communication skills are very strong and she is highly regarded for her contributions to team meetings. However, next week Laura has to make a presentation to the senior management group for the first time. She knows that two of the executives to whom she will be presenting are well known for their harsh views about the sales team as a whole and although Laura has been performing well, she knows that this will not count for much in this particular situation. She is nervous about the presentation and is concerned that she may blow her opportunity for impressing the key decision makers in the organization. At the back of her mind she knows that she can do it but she is becoming increasingly anxious about all the things that could go wrong in the ten minutes she will be on stage presenting.

How could you help Laura? Which aspects of the two critical moment tips might work for her? Again, make some notes in the chart below.

My advice to Laura

Now we have Paul – the IT specialist who is really struggling with road warrior syndrome and needs some Endurance Toughness coaching.

Mental Toughness Scenario 3: Paul – 41-year-old IT specialist

Paul works for a software company that is undergoing significant change with the prospect of a merger in the coming months. Staff reductions have led to a situation whereby he is having to cover two jobs for a three month period. This requires him to have an office base in London and another in Leeds. His travel schedule has become a major issue in recent weeks involving him being away from home far more than he would wish and clocking up many extra miles on the motorways and trains. He is starting to feel chronically tired and run down and seems to be getting more than his fair share of coughs and colds. He is under pressure to add the odd visit to Brussels into his already packed schedule but he is worried that this will push him over the edge. His boss is not overly sympathetic and simply advises him to delegate more and organize his time efficiently. Paul has two colleagues who seem to cope quite well with similar schedules and who often appear far more energetic than he ever feels – contributing more to team meetings and coming up with innovative ideas which have impact. Paul feels that he is simply keeping his head above water.

Where would your focus be in coaching Paul? Make your notes in the chart below as previously.

My advice to Paul

Finally, there is Karen – the buyer who appears unable to confidently seize the day and lacks Risk Management Toughness.

Mental Toughness Scenario 4: Karen – 36-year-old buyer

Karen is a buyer for a retail company in London. She has been in her current role for 3 years and although she is well respected and enjoys working for the organization, she has always felt that her style is overly cautious and that she would raise her performance significantly if she could push herself into difficult situations more often and take some riskier options. She finds it hard to make tough decisions and tends to default to the safe option which invariably delivers acceptable, but not exceptional, performance. She greatly admires one of her colleagues who seems able to make the tough calls and go for the risky option even when the stakes are quite high. Karen has several opportunities coming up in the next few months to adopt a new approach but is not confident that she will 'seize the day'.

How will you help Karen overcome her reluctance to go for it? Capture your thoughts in the final blank chart below to complete your game plan coach challenge.

My advice to Karen

The coaching and advice that you have identified as appropriate for these four individuals will not have covered all the tactics and ideas covered in the book but hopefully the exercise has demonstrated how your knowledge of mental toughness has increased since you began reading the first chapter.

Next steps

Looking back, I think people will consider the 2005 Ashes series as the greatest ever. They will say that the England team had a huge amount of self-belief and showed an enormous amount of character.[1]

Michael Vaughan, Captain of the 2005 Ashes winning England Cricket Team

Despite Michael Vaughan's pride in reflecting on the self-belief and character of his England team, if you reread his words in the Preface of this book you'll see that he is constantly thinking about improving and taking the team to the next level. This is part of the athlete mindset to which I have been referring in Tip 1 and it is a relevant thought upon which to frame this concluding section.

You've just about finished this book and have devised your game plan but where will you go next to keep your performance bar on the rise? Obviously you'll be reviewing your game plan in the coming months and modifying it as appropriate but what else? How can you continue to keep developing your winning approach to mental toughness? I'd like to suggest a couple of options for you to consider – more reading and coaching.

More reading

Many books on business development and self-help exist these days. They're also easy to locate with online purchase companies like Amazon. Simply go to the site and enter your keywords and you'll see various titles covering the topics related to your chosen subject. I've always felt that good books are a cheap investment in your performance development. If you are able to glean just a couple of key pointers from a book that costs £15 that strikes me as being a bargain. Consider how impactful those pointers might be in your performance at work. Imagine the financial implications if you got an idea that enabled you to really nail a sales pitch in a way that you would not have done before. Or if you got a tip about how to lead a more healthy life and as a consequence you contracted fewer illnesses over the course of a year and hence were more productive at work. What about if you read a book that really moves you or inspires you in some really meaningful way? Often these experiences that people have from reading books can stay with them for a lifetime – and all for the cost of less than a business lunch for two!

I feel that many people are put off buying books because they think of them in the way that they view a novel. In other words, they believe that the book must be read from start to finish. Development books are not like that. My office bookshelves are packed with books that I have not read from cover to cover. I have many titles that I have dipped in to over the years, picking up tips and ideas along the way. In fact, I have a philosophy towards book purchase, which is that if I get just one single new idea that I can use in my job then it has been worth the expense. If I get several (which is usually the case) then I view the purchase as a real bargain.

It's also worth considering reading books a second time. Many people find that this is similar to watching a really good movie twice. During the second viewing you often pick up bits that you did not notice the first time around. It's also pretty hard to retain all the ideas and information that are presented in a book with only one reading. So why don't you start by making a pledge to read *The Game Plan* a second time a year from now? You may be surprised how useful this is in keeping you connected with your performance thinking and attitudes.

Coaching

Coaching is a great way of developing your winning approach to mental toughness. It can help you open up to completely new ways of thinking, as well as providing an important sounding board as part of your planning and goal setting processes. You may be in the fortunate position of working for a company which supplies you with a performance coach as part of your development. If this is the case, you're lucky, make the most of it. If not, then why not consider partnering up with a colleague and coach each other? I am a firm believer that peer coaching is an untapped source of potential in most organizations. People tend to think of coaching as either top-down or provided by an outside specialist.

This need not be the case. Over the years of my business consultancy I have observed many extremely powerful coaching relationships develop between peers. The arrangement doesn't have to be formal. Once you've found someone to partner with, then it's simply a matter of arranging a time when you can meet for a coffee or lunch. Simply spend an hour or so talking to each other about the challenges that you are currently facing and bounce ideas around relating to how you can manage things differently.

Coaching relationships are effective at keeping people on track with their goals and action plans. They create a kind of accountability which can serve as a motivating force to stick with your plan. They can also be a much needed source of support whereby individuals can offload worries and ask for help in devising coping strategies especially when under pressure. Of course, levels of trust must be high for the relationship to work effectively so choosing the right partner should be done with care.

It's not just that you will benefit from *receiving* some coaching support. Actually *providing* coaching for someone else is a good way of keeping your awareness levels raised. You have to think of good questions to ask the other person and be ready to comment on their plans and goals. You must be prepared to act as an intelligent sounding board and this requires you to be on top of your game. I have frequently heard business clients explain how they have derived personal benefits from coaching someone else. So basically, it's a win-win situation which I strongly encourage you to explore. Think now about who would be a good person with whom you can partner up. Speak to them as soon as possible and explore how you might create a mutually rewarding coaching relationship. Don't forget though … you don't have to have all the answers to be an effective coach. It's more about asking good questions which both challenge and support.

FINAL WORDS

At the heart of my mental toughness model are *self-belief*, *clear thinking* and *resilience*. If you can develop your winning approach in these three areas you'll be well on the way to being a mentally tough performer. Imagine yourself as having strong and robust self-belief, being able to think clearly when under intense pressure and having the resilience to actually thrive (rather than merely survive) during challenging times. What a great feeling that would be? Well, if you stick to your game plan over the coming months I'm confident that you'll make significant progress. Don't forget to enjoy yourself along the way though. If you can't find fun in what you're doing it's really hard to develop mental toughness. Remember how I explained in the winning environment chapter just how fundamental enjoyment was to Michael Vaughan's leadership philosophy during the Ashes success and Freddie Flintoff certainly embraces this philosophy wholeheartedly.

> *I'm just trying my best, trying to make my way … As far as comparisons with people, I don't see it like that. I'm just playing cricket with my mates and enjoying it.*[2]
>
> **Andrew 'Freddie' Flintoff, on being compared with Ian Botham**

So you now have the knowledge and the tools to take control and do something about your winning approach to mental toughness. Fasten your seatbelt and press down on the accelerator – challenge yourself to change, be open to new ways of thinking, remain eternally optimistic and of course … enjoy the ride!

Notes

Chapter 1

1 Berry, Scyld, *The Sunday Telegraph*, 4.9.05
2 Barnes, Simon, *The Times*, 1.7.99
3 Wilkinson, Jonny, *The Times*, 17.10.05
4 Flintoff, Andrew, *The Times*, 19.9.05
5 In an interview with the author, 2002

Chapter 2

1 Vaughan, Michael, *The Daily Telegraph*, 1.6.04
2 Fletcher, Duncan, *The Times*, 8.1.00
3 Cracknell, James, *The Daily Telegraph*, 11.2.06
4 Halliday, Roy, *USA Today*, 30.6.05
5 Strauss, Andrew, *The Sunday Telegraph*, 20.11.05
6 McKenna, Lesley, *The Daily Telegraph*, 2.2.06
7 Biondi, Matt, in *The Sporting World* by Lynam, D. & Teasdale, D., BBC Books, 1994.
8 Cantona, Eric, in *Cantona on Cantona* by Cantona, E. & Fynn, A., Manchester United Books, 1996
9 Woods, Tiger, *The Sunday Telegraph*, 4.6.00
10 Barnes, Stuart, *The Daily Telegraph*, 28.6.97
11 Goleman, Daniel, *Working with Emotional Intelligence*, Bloomsbury, 1998

Chapter 3

1   Woodward, Clive, *The Sunday Telegraph*, 28.10.01
2   Vaughan, Michael, in *Ashes Victory*, The England Cricket Team, Orion, 2005
3   Vaughan, Michael, in *Michael Vaughan: Calling the Shots*, Hodder & Stoughton, 2005
4   Vaughan, Michael, in *Michael Vaughan: Calling the Shots*, Hodder & Stoughton, 2005
5   Faldo, Nick, *The Times*, 13.3.04
6   Giles, Ashley, *The Wisden Cricketer*, Vol. 2, No. 1, October, 2004
7   Pace, Kate, in *Embracing Your Potential* by Orlick, T., Human Kinetics, 1998
8   Tribble, Curt, in *Remember and forgive, Journal of Performance Education*, Vol. 1, No. 1, 1996
9   Tribble, Curt, in *Remember and forgive, Journal of Performance Education*, Vol. 1, No. 1, 1996

Chapter 4

1   Vaughan, Michael, in *Michael Vaughan: Calling the Shots*, Hodder & Stoughton, 2005
2   Syed, Matthew, *The Times*, 2.6.00
3   In an article by Rosemary Bennett, Deputy Political Editor of *The Times*, 25.10.05
4   Dallaglio, Lawrence, *The Times*, 15.11.97
5   Coomber, Alex, *The Sunday Telegraph*, 17.2.02
6   Thorpe, Graham, *The Daily Telegraph*, 28.1.98
7   Solberg, Petter, *The Daily Telegraph*, 10.11.03
8   Els, Ernie, *The Times*, 12.7.03
9   Benedetti, Nicola, *The Daily Telegraph*, 4.5.04
10 Francona, Terry, *The International Herald and Tribune*, 29.10.04
11 Radcliffe, Paula, BBC TV, 13.4.03

12 Fletcher, Duncan, *Ashes Regained: The Coach's Story*, Simon & Schuster, 2005

13 Floyd, Ray, *From 60 yards In*, Harper Perennial, 1989

14 Gunnell, Sally, *Sally Gunnell: Running Tall*, Bloomsbury, 1994

15 Nicklaus, Jack, in *The Sporting World* by Lynam, D. & Teasdale, D., BBC Books, 1994

16 Hussain, Nasser, in *Manorama Magazine*, June, 2000

17 Eriksson, Sven-Goran, in *Sven-Goran Eriksson on Football*, by Eriksson, S-G, Railo, W., & Matson, H., Carlton Books, 2002

18 Graham, Laurie, in *Psyched: Inner Views of Winning*, by Orlick, T. & Partington, J., Coaching Association of Canada, 1986

19 Ramsay, Gordon, *The Sunday Times*, 11.7.04

20 Slattery, Garry, *The Sunday Times*, 11.7.04

21 Opik, Lembit, *The Sunday Times*, 11.7.04

22 Gunning, Kevin, *The Sunday Times*, 11.7.04

23 Beckham, David, *David Beckham: My Side*, CollinsWillow, 2003

24 Hussain, Nasser, *Playing with Fire*, Penguin Books, 2004

Chapter 5

1 Branson, Richard, in *Beating the 24/7: How business leaders achieve a successful work/life balance*, Wiley, 2002

2 In an interview with the author, 2002

3 Loehr, J. & Schwartz, T. *The Power of Full Engagement: Managing ENERGY, not time, is the key to HIGH PERFORMANCE, HEALTH, and HAPPINESS*, Allen and Unwin, 2003

4 Stone, Sharon, *The Daily Telegraph*, 17.3.06

5 Eccles, Ron, *The Daily Telegraph*, 4.2.06

6 Stewart, Jackie, *Jackie Stewart's Principles of Performance Driving*, Edited by Henry, A., Hazleton Publishing, 1992

7   Flintoff, Andrew, in *Ashes Victory*, The England Cricket Team, Orion, 2005
8   Pringle, Derek, *The Daily Telegraph*, 25.10.05
9   Fletcher, Duncan, *Ashes Regained: The Coach's Story*, Simon & Schuster, 2005
10   Warne, Shane, *The Daily Mail*, 2.8.00
11   Clarke, Darren, *The Daily Telegraph*, 2.4.01
12   Vaughan, Michael, in *Ashes Victory*, The England Cricket Team, Orion, 2005
13   Orlick, Terry, *Embracing Your Potential*, Human Kinetics, 1998
14   Hagen, Walter, in *The Guinness Dictionary of Sports Quotations* by Jarman, C, Guinness Publishing, 1990
15   Vaughan, Michael, *The Daily Telegraph*, 17.12.04
16   Mullaly, Alan, *The Daily Telegraph*, 15.8.00
17   Waugh, Steve, *The Sunday Telegraph*, 12.8.01
18   Thorpe, Graham, *BBC Five Live Radio*, 10.9.02

Chapter 6

1   Kotter, John, *Leading Change*, Harvard Business School Press, 1996
2   Eriksson, Sven-Goran, in *Sven-Goran Eriksson on Football*, by Eriksson, S-G, Railo, W., & Matson, H., Carlton Books, 2002
3   Bowden, Billy, *The Daily Telegraph*, 9.11.05
4   Illingworth, Raymond, in *Ashes Victory*, The England Cricket Team, Orion, 2005
5   Gower, David, in *Ashes Victory*, The England Cricket Team, Orion, 2005
6   Pietersen, Kevin, *The Daily Telegraph*, 10.2.06
7   Faldo, Nick, *The Times*, 13.3.04
8   Wood, Keith, *The Daily Telegraph*, 17.3.06

Chapter 7

1 Trescothick, Marcus, in *Ashes Victory*, The England Cricket Team, Orion, 2005

2 Inverarity, John, *The Daily Telegraph*, 16.4.05

3 Robertson, John, in *The 90 Minute Manager: Business lessons from the dugout*, by Bolchover, D., & Brady, C., Financial Times Prentice Hall, 2002

4 Vaughan, Michael, *The Daily Telegraph*, 1.6.04

5 Vaughan, Michael, in *Ashes Victory*, The England Cricket Team, Orion, 2005

Chapter 9

1 Vaughan, Michael, in *Ashes Victory*, The England Cricket Team, Orion, 2005

2 Flintoff, Andrew, in *Ashes Victory*, The England Cricket Team, Orion, 2005

Index

Contacting the Author

Dr Steve Bull provides executive coaching on a 1-1 basis as well as workshop and development programmes in a variety of areas such as mental toughness, managing pressure, leadership, coaching, team development and culture change. You could also book him as a speaker for one of your corporate events and hear his stories and advice first hand. Visit his website on **www.gameplancoach.com** for further details on how he could provide a consultancy service for your company.